Top 25 locator map
(continues on inside
back cover)

◄

Fodor's
TOKYO'S 25 BEST

by Martin Gostelow

Fodor's Travel Publications
New York • Toronto •
London • Sydney • Auckland
www.fodors.com

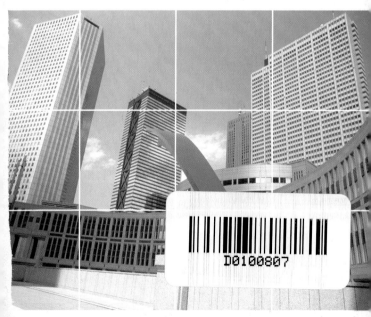

About This Book

ORGANIZATION

This guide is divided into six chapters:

- Planning Ahead, Getting There
- Living Tokyo—Tokyo Now, Tokyo Then, Time to Shop, Out and About, Walks, Tokyo by Night
- Tokyo's Top 25 Sights
- Tokyo's Best—best of the rest
- Where To—detailed listings of restaurants, hotels, shops and nightlife
- Travel Facts—practical information

In addition, easy-to-read side panels provide extra facts and snippets, highlights of places to visit and invaluable practical advice.

The colors of the tabs on the page corners match the colors of the triangles aligned with the chapter names on the contents page opposite.

MAPS

The fold-out map in the wallet at the back of this book is a comprehensive street plan of Tokyo. The first (or only) grid reference given for each attraction refers to this map. **The Top 25 locator map** found on the inside front and back covers of the book itself is for quick reference. It shows the Top 25 Sights, described on pages 28–52, which are clearly plotted by number (**1**–**25**, not page number) across the city. The second map reference given for the Top 25 Sights refers to this map.

Contents

Planning Ahead

WHEN TO GO

Spring is the best time to visit the city, when plum, peach and cherry blossoms are at their best; the golden colors of fall are beautiful. Both spring and fall are also peak holiday times for the Japanese, and the Golden Week (Apr 29–May 5) is very busy. The monsoon season, which brings rain for days on end, begins in June; you should carry an umbrella. The city is virtually closed from Dec 28 to Jan 3.

TIME

Japan is 13 hours ahead of New York, 16 hours ahead of Los Angeles and 9 hours ahead of London GMT.

AVERAGE DAILY MAXIMUM TEMPERATURES

JAN	FEB	MAR	APR	MAY	JUN	JUL	AUG	SEP	OCT	NOV	DEC
48°F	48°F	53°F	65°F	72°F	77°F	84°F	86°F	79°F	70°F	61°F	53°F
9°C	9°C	12°C	18°C	22°C	25°C	29°C	30°C	26°C	21°C	16°C	12°C

Spring (Mar to May) can be warm, particularly in April and May.
Summer (June to August) is hot and humid–maximum 32°C.
Fall (September to November) usually brings clear skies and comfortable temperatures. The rainiest time is mid-September to October.
Winter (December to February) is quite dry and not excessively cold–temperatures rarely drop below freezing. The days are usually brisk and bright, and there are occasional light snowfalls.

WHAT'S ON

January *Dezomeshiki* (Jan 6): Acrobatic displays by firemen on the top of tall bamboo ladders on Chuo-dori, Harumi.
Young Adults' Day: Tens of thousands of 20-year-olds troop to the Meiji Shrine.
February *Setsubun Bean-Throwing Festival* (Feb 3): Held at many shrines and temples to drive away evil.
March *Doll Festival.*
May *Sanja Matsuri*: Three-day festival in mid-month with parades of portable shrines at Asakusa Kannon (Sensoji) Temple.

June *Sanno Matsuri Festival* (Jun 10–16): At Hie Jinja, parades carry shrines through Akasaka.
July *Sumida River Fireworks*: First held in 1773, this is Japan's biggest pyrotechnics display.
August *O-Bon*: Buddhist temple festivals honor the dead with dancing, fireworks and floating lanterns.
October *Oeshiki Festival* (Oct 11–13): Night lantern procession at Hommonji Buddhist Temple.
November *Emperor Meiji's birthday festival* (Nov 3).

Shichi-go-san (Nov 15): Three-, five- and seven- year old children are taken to shrines.
December *Gishi-sai* (evening of Dec 14): Honors the 47 *ronin* at Sengakuji Temple.
Hagoita-ichi (Dec 17–19): Traditional battledore fair and market at Sensoji Temple, Asakusa.
Emperor's Brithday (Dec 23): The Imperial Palace grounds are open.
New Year holiday (Dec 28–Jan 3): Businesses close, along with many attractions.

TOKYO ONLINE

At the heart of Japan's digital culture, Tokyo has an array of English-language websites with regularly updated information on everything from the theater to local news, dining, weather and gossip.

www.club.nokia.co.jp/tokyoq

All that's cool in the megalopolis—events and dining, art and design, and clubs.

www.tcvb.or.jp

The Tokyo Convention and Visitors Bureau's excellent site, with transportation, attractions, festivals, museums and shopping.

www.bento.com/tokyofood.html

The Tokyo Food Page is a complete guide to eating in Tokyo and Japanese cuisine, with receipes and more than 1,000 restaurant listings.

www.tokyoessentials.com

All you need to help plan your Tokyo trip.

www.pandemic.com/tokyo

Eating, sleeping and seeing the city.

www.tokyo.to

The online edition of the English-language Tokyo Journal covers art, movies, music, nightlife, dining and events in the city.

www. yomiuri.co.jp/index-e/htm

The *Daily Yomiuri* website covers politics, the economy and society news.

www.jnto.go.jp

The Japanese National Tourist Organization's site with sensible tips on a stay in the city.

www.japan-guide.com

Articles on Japanese life, the economy, history, entertainment and sports.

www.tourism.metro.tokyo.jp/english

Local government site with tips on self-guiding touring, events and public transportation.

GOOD TRAVEL SITES

www.fodors.com

You can book air tickets, cars and rooms; research prices and weather; pose questions to fellow travelers; and link to other sites.

www.narita-airport.or.jp

The Narita Airport website details flight arrivals and departures, tourist information and what to expect from airport shopping.

CYBERCAFÉS

Cyberia Tokyo

✉ Scala Building 1F, 1-14-17 Nishi-Azabu, Minato-ku ☎ 3423–0318
🕐 Daily 11–11
💴 ¥1,000 per hour

Papyrus

✉ 2F 1-35-8 Asakusa, Taito-ku ☎ 3842–4687
🕐 Mon–Sat 10.30–8
💴 ¥600 per hour

Café 'TnT'

✉ Liberty Ikebukero, B-1, 2-18-1 Ikebukero, Toshima-ku
☎ 5950–9983
🕐 Thu–Tue noon–10pm
💴 ¥800 per hour

Getting There

ENTRY REQUIRMENTS

Citizens of the US, Canada, Netherlands, Australia and New Zealand may stay 90 days without a visa. Citizens of the UK, Republic of Ireland and Germany do not need a visa for stays of up to 180 days. If you do need a visa, your passport must be valid for three months after your entry date.

ARRIVING

Narita, Tokyo's international airport is 40 miles (64km) northeast of the city, served by train, Limousine Bus and taxis. Tokyo's older airport, Haneda (12 miles/20km south of the city), is used by domestic flights and China Airlines flights to and from Taiwan. Flights from London and New York take 12.5 hours.

MONEY

The unit of currency is the yen (¥). Coins in use are ¥1, 5, 10, 50, 100, 500. Banknotes are for ¥1,000, ¥5,000 and ¥10,000.

1,000 yen

2,000 yen

5,000 yen

10,000 yen

ARRIVING BY AIR

Narita International Airport ☎ 0476 34–5000. has extensive Japanese and western dining, and shopping for souvenirs, cameras, electricals and fashion goods. There are two duty-free stores in Terminal 1 and four in Terminal 2.

Airport Limousine (☎ 03 3665–7220) coaches run from Narita Airport to Tokyo City Air Terminal (TCAT) and to major hotels (journey time around 90 minutes; ¥3,000; pick-up outside terminals). JR trains connect the airport with Tokyo Station (55 minutes; ¥3,000) and Shinjuku, said to be the world's biggest and busiest station (80 minutes; ¥3,100); Keisei Railway trains link the airport to Ueno and Higashi-Ginza stations; (1 hour; ¥1,950).

Try not to take a taxi—the fare could be as high as ¥30,000, although sharing the cost will reduce this considerably.

A monorail connects Haneda Airport to Hamamatsu-cho Station on the JR Yamanote Line (20 minutes; ¥290).

GETTING AROUND

Tokyo has an excellent and efficient public transportation system. The rail system, a mix of the government JR line and several private lines, offers regular services, is spotlessly clean, and runs on time. If you have any doubts about destinations or correct departing platforms, rail staff are generally very helpful.

The subway (Metro) is the usual way of getting around in Tokyo but can be very crowded at peak periods. The JR Yamanote rail loop line links important central locations and can be quicker than the subway. Pick up a map of the system at major stations. Each line is identified by a color, used consistently on maps, signs and sometimes on the trains, too. EIDAN and TOEI Metro lines and JR one-day tickets allow unlimited travel but seldom pay for themselves. Purchase a JR iO card and a subway Pass Net to save buying tickets. High-denomination cards yield a small discount. Tickets are not interchangeable between JR, subway and private lines. The Japan Rail Pass—for 7, 14 or 21 days unlimited travel on JR trains—is good value for travel around Japan, for example to Kyoto and back by *shinkansen* ("bullet train"). To aquire this, buy an exchange order outside Japan, and the pick up the pass itself at a main JR ticket counter. If you do this at Narita Airport on arrival, you can use the pass to travel into the city. It is not valid for the Nozomi express train.

Public buses are slower and more confusing than the subway. Destinations, and information at stops, are usually marked only in Japanese characters.

Taxis charge a high rate for the first 2km (just over one mile), ¥660 (and 30 per cent more from 11pm–5am). The fare then rises rapidly. A red light in the front window indicates that a taxi is available. Use the left-hand, curbside door; it opens and closes by remote control. Don't try to do it yourself.

For more information on getting around ▶ 91.

INSURANCE AND HEALTH MATTERS

Check your coverage before traveling and buy a supplementary policy if needed. Japanese hospitals have high standards but are expensive. No vaccinations are required to enter Japan.

DRIVING IN TOKYO

Congestion, difficult parking and Japanese-only signs make it inadvisable for visitors to drive. If you must do so, obtain an International Driving Permit before arrival in Japan, and bring your local license as well. Tokyo has an extensive system of freeways, but tolls are high. Traffic keeps to the left.

VISITORS WITH DISABILITIES

Tokyo is not the easiest city for visitors in wheelchairs because the subway system has few elevators or escalators; trains are crowded; and people tend to dash around. But many new buildings have excellent facilities for disabled visitors, and there are some special walkways for sight-impaired pedestrians.

Living
Tokyo

Tokyo Now

Above: Cinema complex in Tokyo

Right: Commuters boarding a train in the Tokyo rush hour

Gray and monotonous at first sight, Tokyo soon comes into focus as a pastiche of self-contained districts. Each one—just minutes from one another on the subway system—is like a separate town or village with its own distinctive flavor. Glitzy Ginza attracts the wealthy and tourists who come to see them. Asakusa, with its Sensoji temple, is the spiritual home of older locals.

SALARYMAN

• Recession is greatly changing working patterns in Japan. Yet the salaryman is still a typical figure. He's the man in the dark suit and white shirt that you see on the subway or hurrying to the office. He'll work until 7pm, then go to a bar to drink, smoke and snack with the people he's been with all day. He and his boss may sing karaoke together, or even talk frankly, and he may not get home until after midnight. Salaryman joined the company straight from college and although the old idea of a job for life is fading fast, hopes to spend his career climbing the corporate ladder. However, on both sides, the assumption remains that salaryman will stay with his company until he retires.

ETIQUETTE

• The intricate local rules of etiquette do not apply to visitors to Japan. However, to please your hosts, always take your shoes off when entering a house or room with straw matting. And remember that a slight bow is good form after you buy something in a shop or when meeting people.

A young boy in front of a temple in Tokyo

Ueno, in the north, claims some excellent museums and budget shopping. The young relax in Shibuya and Ikebukuro; for shopping, they stroll tree-lined Dogonzaka toward the trendy Aoyama 1-Chrome district. Ometesando -dori, in the Harajuku area, is the local Champs Élysées, with its many Parisian-style outdoor cafés. Shinjuku is known for its fleshpots and seedy bars. Expats and locals alike head to Roppongi for a lively night out.

Some districts' characters change during the day or the week. After dark, elaborate neon signs transform parts of Tokyo. Flashing signs and glowing lanterns in 100,000 restaurants and drinking dens beckon, and your dining

11

Above: *Young shopper*
Above right: *Neon-lit streets*
Right: *Young businessmen relaxing in Hibiya Park*

NEIGHBORHOODS

• Tokyo and its suburbs, home to around 12 million people, sprawl across the Kanto Plain on Japan's largest island, Honshu. The metropolitan area is divided into 23 wards (*ku*)—of which most visitors see only five or six around central Tokyo. Within these wards are districts that, for the purposes of this book, are defined according to their major attractions.

choices are limited only by your budget. Toward midnight, entertainment districts are full of cheerful revelers heading for the last train home to sleep it off before the work day begins again. And on weekends, families congregate in the suburban parks with their obviously much adored children.

Few old or historic buildings remain in Tokyo; the city experienced a recession after a massive 1923 earthquake and the World War II fire bombing, which left the city in ruins. Now new hotels, office and apartment blocks are springing up and the city's skyline is modern and stylish. Yet charming corners turn up here and there: An equisite art collection is hidden away on the top floor of an anonymous office tower; a tranquil shrine nestles in the shadow of an elevated expressway; a stupendous collection of bonsai plants turns up in a suburban office building. You are always aware of the seasons: Winter, with its frosts and the

occasional snowfall; spring bringing blossoms in parks and gardens; and fall, turning the leaves gold on every tree.

Traditional dress has also faded from Tokyo's landscape. While many older women dress in kimonos—probably off to a special occasion—

THE OFFICE LADY

• A woman is traditionally not expected to have a career. To fill in the years until she gets married, she might work as an *oeru* (office lady or OL— pronounced "o-eru"). While men take the 'real' jobs, the oeru shuffles paper, pours tea and looks pretty. But she exacts a sort of revenge: Unlike the young salaryman, who has to spend his spare money partying with colleagues, the oeru can save her money to take foreign holidays. With western pressures and influences encouraging younger Japanese women to be much more assertive and to enjoy life, even as a single woman, the oeru's horizons may become so wide that her male counterpart seems gauche and inexperienced by comparison.

WOMAN IN ORBIT

• Former science minister Makiko Tanaka's talk with Chiaki Mukai, the first Japanese woman astronaut, during the 15 days she spent orbiting in a US space shuttle in 1994, represented twin pinnacles of achievement for Japanese womanhood. A heart surgeon, Mukai is a heroine to many women who feel that society has not allowed them to reach their full potential.

13

Above: *Fast-food Tokyo-style*
Right: *A panoramic view across the rooftops of Tokyo, from a skyscraper in the Akakusa district*

most of the city's women wear western fashions, and older men dress in fashionable American or European garb. Young women, especially, wear the most outlandish gear, including funky, colorful clothes and platform shoes. To see them at their most eye-opening, head for Harajuku on any weekend.

Tokyoites have an immediately apparent fetish for order and fastidious cleanliness. Patience

HOME BOYS

- It is estimated that as many as one million young Japanese, mostly male, live a reclusive life known as *hikikomori*, staying at home supported by their parents, well into their thirties. While some can manage a trip to local shops, others barely leave their bedrooms, and spend their days surfing the Web or watching television. Psychologists ascribe the condition to an unwillingness to engage in Japanese "groupism," one of the driving forces of the nation's economic power, a reaction to having been bullied in school. The condition is proving a drain on the economy and further pressure on an already low birthrate.

A temple in Tokyo

and self-control are instilled from birth and reinforced by example. Constantly moving crowds conduct themselves with remarkable efficiency. The infinitely courteous local police look after their neighborhoods, on foot, on bicycle, or on duty in roadside huts. People take care of their own space, both at home and at work. The silence on the rush-hour commuter trains can be almost weird, and the sight of around half the commuters asleep on their way to work belies the hectic lifestyle. People are calm and seem to transmit their mood to those who join them, even in a subway car that's body-to-body.

Tokyo remains one of the most monocultural of all world capitals. The city, like the nation whose capital it is, feels like a world of its own. Outside the realms of business and tourism, English isn't widely spoken, yet lost travelers will find the locals both extremely friendly and most helpful.

FACTS AND FIGURES

● Over five million people travel to work daily.

● There are over five million motor vehicles in the city, at least two million in use on any given day.

● Life expectancy is age 84 for women and age 77 for men (among the world's highest).

● There are more restaurants per capita than anywhere else in the world.

Tokyo Then

Above: Kabuki *performance*
Above right: *Tombs of some of the 47 ronin (loyal subjects) buried in the grounds of the Sengakuji Temple in the Takanawa district*

THE PILOT AND THE *SHOGUN*

In April 1600, the lone surviving ship of a Dutch trading fleet reached Japan, crewed by a mere six men. One was an English pilot, Will Adams. He was taken to meet Ieyasu, who was eager to learn about European ways and who asked Adams to build him a ship. The pilot ("Anjin-san") spent the rest of his life serving the *shoguns*, dying in 1620. Readers of James Clavell's novel *Shogun* will recognize the story, although names were changed and many details invented.

250–710 Kofun Culture. From 300 to 400 unification under Yamato clan. Yamato power declines 400–600. Spread of Buddhism.

794 Imperial capital moves from Nara to Kyoto.

850–1150 Rise of the *samurai* (warrior) class and rapid spread of Buddhism.

1192 *Shoguns* are victorious in a power struggle. Yoritomo Minamoto rules from Kamakura as *shogun*.

1336 Ashikaga Takauji takes over as *shogun*—establishes his rule in Kyoto.

1572– 1600 The warlord Nobunaga Oda seizes power in Kyoto. After Oda was murdered in 1582, Hideyoshi Toyotomi unites the country. On his death in 1598, a power struggle ensues.

1600–39 Ieyasu Tokugawa is victorious at the battle of Sekigahara. The Tokugawa *shogunate* is established.

1853/58 The Treaty of Kanagawa, signed in 1858, opens ports to trade.

1867–68 After a coup d'état against the *shogunate*; Emperor Meiji installed. Edo is renamed Tokyo ("Eastern Capital"). Shinto is declared the state religion.

1894– 1910	War with China and Russia. In 1910 Japan annexes Korea.
1923	An earthquake in the city kills about 140,000.
1926	Hirohito becomes emperor.
1930s	The military increasingly dominate the government. Japan invades China.
1945–52	US General Douglas MacArthur rules after Japan surrenders at the end of the war. Emperor Hirohito renounces his claim to divine status. Japanese independence is restored in 1952.
1960s	Rapid economic and industrial recovery. Tokyo hosts Olympic Games in 1964.
1980s	Japan becomes the world's greatest trading nation. Tokyo's stock market booms. Emperor Akihito succeeds Hirohito in 1989.
1991–94	Recession. The stock market falls by 60 percent.
1995	An earthquake devastates Kobe.
2000	The economy continues to stagnate amid record unemployment and bankruptcies.
2005	Tokyo construction boom.

Above left: *Detail of a woodblock print of a Ninja warrior*
Above: *Detail of swirling, gilded dragons decorating the interior of the Higashi Hongwanji Buddhist Temple*

WORLD WAR II

In December 1941 Japan attacked Pearl Harbor, and the US entered World War II. Defeat by the US navy in the Battle of Midway marked the turning point of the war. In 1944–45 air raids leveled much of Tokyo. On two nights in March 1945, much of the city was destroyed by fire and around 100,000 died and a million homes destroyed. Atomic bombs were dropped on Hiroshima (440 miles/ 708km from Tokyo) and Nagasaki (610 miles/ 981km) from Tokyo) despite Japan's imminent surrender.

17

Time to Shop

Shop early, shop often! Tokyo is a shopper's paradise and for the locals it is serious business. The place to begin shopping in Tokyo is at the large department stores. Here you'll find floors of

merchandise that is beautifully designed and in extreme good taste. Look out especially for fashion goods, homewares, including exquisite ceramics, lacquerware and soft furnishings, and arts and crafts such as the minature dolls. These stores are located in most precincts and shopping areas (► 74).

Since the Japanese invented consumer electronics, the products that we can no longer live without, Tokyo is a good place to look for (or at) the latest electronic gadgetry. You might begin at one of the many technology showrooms, such as the Sony Building (► 44) in Ginza.

While it may be a case of look but don't buy in some of Ginza's up-market shops, such as Mikimoto (► 78), many specialty shops, especially in the back streets, have reasonably priced clothing, including kimonos, lovely paper products, traditional fans and way-out designer goods. In fact, a good rule for Tokyo shopping,

COMIC CULT

Perhaps the wierdest craze in Japan is the nation's obsession with *manga*, the comic books of all genres that rail commuters engross themselves in. This has led to *anime*, or animation, the film equivalent that manifests itself in a variety of television and film products, including Astroboy and Akira.

since addresses are often impossible to find, is to wander the back-streets of Shinjuku, Shibuya, Ginza, Ikebukuro and Asakusa in search of your own treasures.

Below left: Young Tokyoites love to shop for clothes
Below: Fish market

TAKESHITA STREET

Street markets such as those found near Ueno station are good places to get a general idea of Japanese merchandise. As you browse the hundreds of stands you'll be among local shoppers who may be looking for something new to wear on the weekend or just choosing dinner from the huge array of seafood, vegetables, dried foods and prepared meals. Food is an important component of any shopping precinct and the Japanese love of packaging makes prepared food items a very tempting retail adventure. The variety, freshness and quality, not to mention tastiness, of what's on offer defies belief; from sushi to tempura, noodle meals (*soba* and *udon*) to luscious, if expensive *unagi* (eel) dishes.

The best flea markets (► 77) are a good place to shop for antiques, although you're unlikely to find bargains. They are, however, great places to learn about Japanese wares, art, old kimonos and assorted bric-a-brac and to purchase something from the old days as a memento.

Takeshita Street is a paradigm of youth culture. There is nowhere quite like this busy shopping street beginning just opposite Harajuku Station near the famed Omotesando dori. The narrow lane is crammed with shops selling fashion to Japanese teenagers—arguably the world's most avid consumers (from imported brand-name labels to obscure local fashion labels that are found nowhere else in the world). In the streets around here on weekends the young dress in the most outlandish gear, so have your camera ready.

19

Out and About

MORE IDEAS...

City Tours
Morning, afternoon and evening tours are offered, as well as all-day packages including lunch. Some tours include a lunchtime boat trip on Tokyo Bay or demonstrations of Japanese flower-arranging or doll-making, or a tea ceremony. An Industrial Tokyo tour may take you to Japan Airlines maintenance base at Haneda Airport, the Kirin Brewery or the Isuzu car factory.

Kenchoki Temple, one of 65 Buddhist temples in and around Kamakura, former capital city of Japan

ORGANIZED TOURS

Tokyo sightseeing tours are somewhat expensive—roughly ¥5,000 for a half-day, ¥12,000 for a full day with lunch, ¥10,000 for a night tour with dinner. Tour companies pick up at main hotels and leave you in Ginza at the

tour's end. You can check on options and prices at hotel desks or the TIC (► 92) Tour companies include Japan Gray Line Co. Ltd B3-3-3 Nishi-Shinbashi, Minato-ku (☎ 3433–5745) and Sunrise Tours, Japan Travel Bureau Incorporated (✉ 2-3–11 Higashishin-agawa, Shinagawa-ku ☎ 5796–5454).

EXCURSIONS
KAMAKURA

INFORMATION

KAMAKURA
Distance 30 miles (48km)
Journey Time about 1 hour
🚉 Kita-kamakura or Kamakura from Tokyo Station, lower level Track 1 (JR Yokosuka Line), or at intermediate stops, Shinbashi or Shinagawa. Hase by local train from Kamakura.

The military ruler Minamoto Yoritomo set up his base at the seaside town of Kamakura in 1192, leaving the emperor as a figurehead in Kyoto. Kamakura remained the seat of power until 1333. Its many shrines and temples are quite spread out, but you can use the train, which has stops within a short distance of the various temples, to cut down the walking. One of Japan's most important temples, the 13th-century Engakuji Temple, is near to Kita-kamakura Station. The Hase Kannon Temple houses the 37-ft (11.4-m) Great Buddha, cast in bronze in 1252. Hase-dera Temple, near Hase station, has a lovely garden. The beach, 15 minutes' walk from the station, is popular in summer.

HAKONE

The mountainous area west of Tokyo, with lakes and countless hot springs, is a favorite weekend destination of local day-trippers. Visit midweek to avoid crowds. From Hakone-Yumoto, the Hakone Tozan Railroad zigzags over the

mountains, making many stops. At Miyanoshita, a resort with thermal pools and mountain walks, stop for lunch or tea at the historic Fujiya Hotel. Next to Chokoku-no-Mori Station is Hakone Open Air Museum, a spectacular sculpture garden and gallery. From the last station, Gora, a cable car soars over Owakudani Valley, where sulphurous fumes and smoke pour from a dozen crevices and you can buy eggs boiled in the hot springs. Another 25 minutes by cable car is Togendai, the base for cruises on Lake Ashi.

MOUNT FUJI (FUJI-YAMA)

For most visitors, a view of the perfect volcanic cone is enough, especially as reflected in Lake Ashi. If you want to see it close up, head for Kawaguchiko, 4 miles (6km) away. Gogome, closer still, is the main starting point for people making the 4- to 5-hour trip to the summit 12,385ft (3,776m) up. The climb can be made only in July and August, and even then weather can be bad, so be prepared with warm clothing, and always be sure to check the weather conditions before attempting the trek.

INFORMATION

HAKONE
Distance 54 miles (90km)
Journey Time 1½hours, then local train (55 mins)
🎨 Open Air Museum daily 9–5, Mar–Oct; 9–4, rest of year
🚆 Hakone–Yumote (Limited Express from Shinjuku Station, Odakyu Line)
💰 Expensive
❓ On Hakone Tozan Railroad, a Hakone Free Pass (not free) covers 4 days' travel by trains, buses, cable car and boats

Mount Fuji

INFORMATION

MOUNT FUJI
Distance 60 miles (100km)
Journey Time 2 hours
☎ English language information line/weather: 0555-72-0259
🚆 Kawaguchiko (Odakyu Line from Shinjuku Station; change at Otsuki)
❓ Tours; buses from Shinjuku to Kawaguchiko

Out and About

INFORMATION

Distance 319 miles (513km)

Journey time 2 hours 30 minutes by bullet train (*shinkansen*)

✉ Tourist Information Centre (TIC): Kyoto Station (9F)

☎ TIC: 075–343–6655

⊙ Daily 8.30–7

🍴 Plenty at station, in city and near major shrines

🚉 Kyoto (from Tokyo Station)

❓ Tours from Tokyo and within Kyoto. Avoid weekends and holiday periods. Arrange accommodations in advance, or call the TIC booking service
☎ 075–752–0227

A monk talking to visitors in a Kyoto temple garden

BAMBOO FOREST

At Arashiyama in western Kyoto, this popular walk meanders through a peaceful forest of tall bamboo. The trail leads to the Nonomiya shrine, which is surrounded by moss gardens.

🚉 JR Sugano Line from Kyoto Station to Saga Arashiyama

KYOTO

Regarded as the spiritual home of the Japanese people, Kyoto steadfastly maintans the essence of Japanese art and culture. Just to the south-west of Toyko, the city is known for its seasonal festivals and theater productions, hundreds of

imposing temples and shrines, delicious tofu-based cuisine and traditional handicrafts. Classical Japanese arts such as the tea ceremony and flower arrangement and the highly popular Geisha districts are other major attractions.

At the Nishinjin Textile Center, specializing in the manufacture of fabrics for the kimono and obi (sashes), you can take in a free Kimono Fashion Show, view weaving and silk painting demonstrations, and admire the many beautiful craft items, traditional sweets and teas for sale on the premises. The Kyoto Handicraft Center, a popular tax-free shop for foreign tourists, sells prints, dolls, dyed and woven crafts, porcelain and pottery. An interesting one-hour overview of tradtional Japanese entertainment—ancient court music and dance, Kyomai dance (performed by apprentice Geisha), Kyogen comedy and Bonraku puppetry is offered at Gion Corner—and after the show, you can master the intricacies of the tea ceremony. Be sure to visit the Nishiki Food Market, with over 120 shops selling fresh produce and seafood.

The Kyoto National Museum has fine art and archeological collections and you can tour the imposing grounds and gardens of the Imperial Palace (reservations essential, be sure to take your passport). Also of interest is Nijo Castle built in 1603 by the last Tokugawa shogun.

Most temples and shrines lie on the city's outskirts, but are easily accessible. The Kiyomizu Temple, beautifully positioned on a hillside, has a wide veranda, with views over the city–its bright vermilion pagoda is a landmark. The buildings of the Heian Shrine and its massive red *torii* gateway, echo the style of the first Imperial Palace in Kyoto. The gardens are famous for their spring blossoms and fall colors. The Ashikaga Shogun Yoshimitsu used the Kinkakuji Temple (Temple of the Golden Pavilion) as a retreat, but after his death the building became a temple. The beautiful gilded structure is set in a traditional Japanese garden. Renowned for its Zen-style garden, with its raked gravel patterns and carefully positioned rocks, the Ryoanji Temple dates from 1450. The shogun, Ashikaga Yoshimasa, who popularized the tea ceremony, built the Ginkakuji Temple (Temple of the Silver Pavilion) in 1482; its gardens famed for their ascetic formality and balance. The nearby Path of Philosophy follows a scenic canal. Works of art are housed in the Toji Temple where a giant temple flea market is held on the 21st of every month.

INFORMATION

Enjoy a 360-degree view over the city and surroundings from Kyoto Tower located in front of Kyoto Station.
🕐 Daily 9am–9pm

KYOTO STATION

The gateway to the city and one of Japan's largest stations, this massive modern building includes a department store, theater, hotel, shops and many restaurants.

The huge torii *at the entrance to Heian Shrine*

KYOTO TRANSPORT

The city is bigger than it looks.

● **Walking** is delightful. A walking guide to Kyoto and vicinity is available from the TICs.

● **Bicycles** are a good way to get around: ask at the TIC.

● **Subways** runs north–south and east–west, but it's more convenient to take a bus.

● **Trains** connect some sights.

● **Public buses** cover all areas. TIC has a route map.

● **Tour buses** are expensive but a good way to see major sights.

23

Walks

INFORMATION

Distance 4 miles (7km)
Time 2½ hours
Start point ★ Asakusa river bus pier
N2
🚇 Asakusa (Ginza and Asakusa lines)
End point Inaricho subway station
🚇 B10
🚇 Inaricho (Ginza Line), or continue along Asakusa-dori to Ueno

The forecourt of Asakusa Kannon Temple in the heart of Asakusa district in downtown Tokyo, the oldest temple in the city

A WALK AROUND ASAKUSA & KAPPABASHI

At the river bus pier from the exit of Asakusa subway station, look across the Sumida River at the dramatic Asahi Brewery buildings designed by Philippe Starck in 1989.

Two blocks west of the river is Kaminarimon, one of the gates to Sensoji (or Asakusa Kannon) Temple. Through it is the pedestrian Nakamise-dori, a street lined with small shops. Take note of the street to the left, Denboin-dori, before touring the temple. Return to Denboin-dori, which leads to the entertainment district, with theaters and places to eat. The Nakase restaurant (► 67), on the first corner, is noted for tempura. Many inexpensive noodle shops are on the side streets. Hanayashiki, behind the temple, is a children's amusement park.

Cut through to the west to the Asakusa View tower on the broad Kokusai-dori. Turn left and follow Kokusai-dori for one block and then turn right onto Asakusa-dori for 300 yards (300 metres), past two temples, to meet the main street of Kappabashi, famous for its stores selling plastic imitation food. Turn left (south) and continue to Asakusa-dori, marked by a giant chef's head. A right turn leads to Inaricho subway station.

INFORMATION

Distance 5 miles (8km)
Time 2½ hours
Start point ★ Ueno JR Station
🚇 L2
🚋 Ueno (Yamanote Line)
🚇 Ueno (Ginza Line),
End point Nezu subway station
🚇 K1
🚋 Nezu
❓ Museums in Ueno Park closed Mon (or Tue if Mon is a national holiday)

Ueno Park

A WALK AROUND UENO & YANAKA

Ueno is one of the city's busiest hubs. The east exit from Ueno's JR station leads to Showa-dori, in the shadow of an elevated expressway. Turn left (north) and you will quickly be in so-called "motorcycle heaven" (► 74). Retrace your steps to the main road junction south of the station and look for the archway leading to Ameyoko, one of Tokyo's liveliest markets, with stalls stretching as far as Okachimachi JR Station. At the market's Ueno end, cross Chuo-dori and enter Ueno Park at its southeast corner, where the Shitamachi folk museum faces Shinobazu Pond, filled with waterfowl. There is more to see in the park, including many shrines and museums, and a zoo featuring giant pandas (► 64).

Yanaka bric-a-brac shop

North of Ueno Park, west of the railroad line, is Yanaka, whose narrow streets and old shops and houses escaped both the 1923 earthquake and 1945 bombing. With its dozens of temples and gardens, this is more like Kyoto than Tokyo. You may well get lost, but it doesn't matter as you will eventually bump into either the Yanaka cemetery (north of Tokyo Museum) on the area's eastern end or Nippori JR Station to the north, and you can get your bearings. Finish at Nezu subway station on the western edge of Yanaka.

Tokyo by Night

Above: *Workers usually end their day with a visit to a bar*
Above right: *Traditional Japanese entertainment*

DRINK PRICES

Drinks at some bars range from very expensive (up to ¥10,000 at a hostess bar) to inexpensive or moderate, ¥500 at a *aka-chochin* or *nomiya*, the small red lantern bars that are everywhere. In between are pub-like *yakitori-ya*, Japanese-style places where you can get food, beer and sake.

GEISHA EVENING

Sunrise Tours offer a two and a half hour evening of traditional Japanese cuisine with entertainment by 'Geisha', including singing and dancing. Most geisha do not speak English. The fee, around ¥50,000, includes hotel transfers. ☎ 5796–5454

Tokyo really comes to life at night. Restaurants offering traditional meals, little eating places where cuisine triumphs over the surroundings, late-opening nightclubs where fusion music is taken to new extremes and bars filled with karaoke-singing revelers are all part of the Tokyo experience. For main entertainment districts ➤ 82.

GOING SOLO
Western visitors to Tokyo who want a night on the town generally head to the Roppongi area, whose dance clubs, bars and pubs attract local expats (*gaijin*) and Japanese alike and where the action continues until the wee hours. Shibuya attracts a younger crowd, and there are any number of live music venues—best discovered by checking a website such as www.club.nokia.co.jp/tokyoq on the day.

NIGHT TOURS
If you are a bit tentative about venturing out at night, consider a night tour. These generally combine dinner with a show and a drive through of Ginza or Akasaka, with their dramatic displays of neon signage. You have a choice of menus, perhaps sukiyaki, *kushiage* (deep-fried morsels on sticks) or steak; the show is usually Kabuki theater or traditional geisha entertainment of music, song and conversation although true geishas don't speak English. Also popular are dinner cruises on Tokyo Bay that give you some great views of the Rainbow Bridge, Fuji TV and Disney Resort by night.

TOKYO's
top 25 sights

The sights are shown on the maps on the inside front cover and inside back cover, numbered **1**–**25** from west to east across the city

Metropolitan Government Offices

HIGHLIGHTS

- The 45th-floor observatories, 663ft (202m) high
- Surreal skyscrapers of Shinjuku
- Views of parks and distant downtown area
- Glimpse of Mount Fuji (1 day in 5)
- Sunset and night views
- Multiscreen video history
- Sculptures in plaza
- Granite exterior—white from Spain, dark from Sweden

INFORMATION

http://www.metro.tokyo.jp

- C4; Locator map A2
- Tokyo Metropolitan Government Offices, 2-8-1 Nishi-Shinjuku, Shinjuku-ku
- 5321–3077
- Daily 9.30am–10pm; closed Dec 29–Jan 3
- Snack bar on 45th floor; restaurants nearby
- Shinjuku
- Shinjuku Tochomae
- Very good
- Free
- Shinjuku Station (▶ 29)

Above: The twin towers of the Metropolitan Government Offices

These striking, grandiose towers and their plazas were planned in the booming 1980s, and opened in 1991. On a clear day the view from the top is unrivaled, with impressive silver and black towers rising all around.

Vantage point Each of the twin towers of Building No. 1 has an observatory on the 45th floor. It makes no difference which tower you choose: The lifts whisk you to the top in less than a minute. On a clear day the view is the most spectacular in Tokyo, with futuristic skyscrapers in the foreground, the green islands of the Meiji Shrine Inner Garden and Shinjuku Garden beyond, and the Imperial Palace, Ginza and Tokyo Bay to the east. If you are lucky, you'll see Mount Fuji's perfect cone far away on the southwestern horizon. The tourist information center on the first floor is open 9.30–6.30 daily, giving you the chance to pick up some useful tips for your trip.

Growth area In the days of the *shogunate*, Shinjuku was still a day's march from the capital, Edo (now Tokyo). Weary travelers coming from the west would stop at its inns to bathe and rest, dine and visit one of the many houses of pleasure. With the coming of the railroad, Shinjuku became a major junction. As late as 1970, Shinjuku was known mainly for its station, red-light district and sewage treatment works. When investors looked for alternatives to central Tokyo, Shinjuku had an important advantage: it seemed to survive earthquakes better than other areas. When the city government decided to move to Shinjuku it commissioned Kenzo Tange to design a new complex to house the offices, on a scale to match its multi-trillion-yen annual budget.

Shinjuku Station

Twice a day, a tidal wave of humanity pours through Japan's busiest station—three to four million commuters, shoppers and schoolchildren stream along its passages, heading for a dozen exits, and changing trains.

Human anthill Subway lines and JR railroad-lines meet at Shinjuku; private lines feed customers to their own department stores right above the station. The famous people-pushers operate at rush hour (*rashawa* in Japanese), packing as many bodies as they can into each carriage, giving them a final shove to let the doors close and then bowing as the train pulls out. It's worth experiencing—once—but not as an introduction to the system. Learn your way around at a quieter time first.

Exits You can walk more than half a mile (1km) underground (more if you get lost). One long concourse on the west side links the station complex to many of Shinjuku's skyscrapers, including the Metropolitan Government Offices. Here and there, the homeless, who have somehow dropped through the cracks of Japan's tightly knit society, find a place to sleep, cocooned in cardboard cartons. To the hurrying crowds they seem invisible. The east exit leads to the My City building with several stories of good eating places and into a maze of alleys and the varied night entertainment of Kabukicho.

HIGHLIGHTS

- Organized chaos of rush hour
- People-pushers
- My City restaurant complex
- Department stores above station
- Underground city
- Harangues by fringe groups of far right and left
- Camera stores near station
- Takashimaya Times Square development on south side of station
- Kabukicho nightlife

INFORMATION

- D4; Locator map A2
- Shinjuku-ku
- 4.30am–11.30pm
- Innumerable eating places of every kind
- Shinjuku
- Shinjuku
- Few
- Free
- Metropolitan Government Offices (➤ 28), Kabukicho (➤ 82)

Clear directions help you find your way around Shinjuku Station

Shinjuku National Garden

HIGHLIGHTS

- Beautifully landscaped garden
- Ponds, bridges and shaded glades
- Japanese garden
- French garden
- English garden
- Greenhouse of tropical plants and flowers
- Chrysanthemum shows
- Fall colors
- Picnic parties under the spring blossoms

INFORMATION

www.shinjukugyoen.go.jp/eng lish/english-index

- E5; Locator map B2
- 11 Naitocho, Shinjuku-ku
- 3350–0151
- Tue–Sun 9–4; closed Mon except at cherry-blossom time
- Snacks
- Shinjuku Gyoen-mae. Take the south exit and turn right
- Shinjuku
- Few
- Moderate
- Shinjuku Station (▶ 29)

Expansive and verdant, the 150-acre (60-ha) Shinjuku National Garden is the perfect place for a stroll especially in April when thousands come to walk and picnic under some 2,000 of their beloved flowering cherry trees.

Origins Shinjuku garden is one of the surpisingly large green spaces that relieve the concrete monotony of the city. It was once the estate of the powerful leader (*daimyo*) of the Naito clan—one of the Tokugawa *shoguns* who parceled out the land around their Edo stronghold to lesser lords whose duty was to defend the approaches. Following the overthrow of the *shogunate* and restoration of the imperial power in 1868, it came into the hands of the emperor. After World War II, it was opened to the public as a national park.

Garden sights Landscaped with little hills, ponds and bridges, the park includes greenhouses filled with tropical plants, an English country garden, a French formal garden and a Japanese garden with a Chinese-style pavilion.

Each year at cherry-blossom time large crowds—guided by the daily blossom reports on TV—are drawn to see almost 2,000 trees, their white or pink petals blowing like snow in the wind. The biggest, most perfect blooms of Japan's national flower, the chrysanthemum, are on show September to November.

The English garden in Shinjuku National Garden

Meiji Jingu Shrine

Walk through the woods to the national focus of the Shinto religion. Here, people mark important stages of their lives. Babies are brought for their first temple visit and newlyweds come to have marriages blessed.

The shrine The reign of Emperor Meiji (1868–1912) saw Japan transformed from a medieval to a modern state. The shrine was built in 1920 to honor him and his empress: In accordance with the beliefs of the day they had been declared divine. The shrine was destroyed by fire in 1945 air raids, but rebuilt in the original classical design. The great *torii* (gates) are made from 1,700-year-old cypress trees from Taiwan. The 150-acre (70-ha) inner gardens are noted for more than 100,000 trees, sent from all over Japan when the gardens were created in 1920. The Treasure Museum at the northern end of the gardens houses royal clothes and possessions.

Occasions Babies dressed in their best are usually brought by proud parents on Thursdays, and you can often see wedding processions— some in traditional costume and some in Western dress. The main festival is on November 3, Emperor Meiji's birthday.

HIGHLIGHTS

- 175 acres (70 ha) of wooded park
- Giant *torii* (gates)
- Shrine hall of cypress wood
- Folded paper prayers on bushes
- Cherry blossoms in spring
- Iris garden in summer
- Winter ice carvings
- Treasure Museum
- Wedding processions

INFORMATION

- ✚ D6; Locator map A3
- ✉ 1-1 Yoyogi, Shibuya-ku
- ☎ 3379–5511
- ⏱ Sunrise–sunset; closed third Fri of each month
- 🚇 Meijijingu-mae
- 🚉 Harajuku, Sangubashi
- ♿ Few 🎫 Free
- ➡ Harajuku (▶ 32), Yoyogi Park (▶ 32), Ota Museum (▶ 55), Japanese Sword Museum (▶ 56)

Harajuku

INFORMATION

Crowds of people clustered around market stands in the popular Yoyogi Park Sunday market in Harajuku

The street scene in this neighborhood is a bizarre parade of the young and would-be young in miniskirts and platform shoes even in winter. Hair is bleached blond or dyed a bright, shocking color.

East of the station Across the street from Harajuku Station, Takeshita-dori is a magnet for teenagers, an alley lined by stalls selling colored glasses, music tapes, fast food, coffee and clothing at prices that are bargains, at least by Tokyo standards. Running parallel is the tree-lined Omotesando-dori, the street that Tokyoites think of as their Champs Élysées, lined with elegant, expensive boutiques. The Ota Museum (► 55), just off it, houses a superb collection of *ukiyo-e* (woodblock prints; ► 55, panel). One of the city's best antiques and flea markets held on the first and fourth Sundays of each month, is just to the north, off Meiji-dori, near the Togo Shrine (► 59). The shrine itself honors Admiral Togo who was the architect of the Japanese navy that defeated the Russian fleet in 1905.

Yoyogi Park The green space west of the station and next to the gounds of Meiji Jingu Shrine was an army camp during World War II, and afterwards the base of US occupying forces. It was also the site of the 1964 Olympic Games village and retains the sports arenas built there. A few years ago the noisy rock bands and street dancers that on Sundays used to fill Inogashira-dori, south of the park, were banned. Across the now quiet road is the National Yoyogi Sports Center and Stadium, designed for the Olympics by Kenzo Tange. The structure's swooping, steel-suspension roof evokes the appearance of those on traditional Japanese temples.

Roppongi Hills

This stunning new precinct, with its central 54-story (780ft/238m) main tower building, includes an urban art gallery, dramatic observation deck, brand-name shops, public art, tranquil open spaces and busy plazas.

Grand scale Covering approximately 4.5 acres (11 ha), with a total floor area of 7,790,240 sq ft (724,000sq m), Roppongi Hills is Japan's largest urban redevelopment project. The complex was designed by Fumihiko Maki as mid-town Tokyo's cultural urban center and a symbol of contemporary Japan. By cleverly integrating office, residential, hotel, retail and cultural facilities with parks and plazas, the architect has drawn locals, expatriates and visitors in droves to this complex that surprises and delights at every turn. A shopping and dining plaza links directly to Roppongi subway station, while a mixed-use building offers commericial and educational facilities, the 390-room five-star Grand Hyatt Tokyo, TV Asahi's broadcasting center and a theater for the performing arts. Shopping options include all the top designer names—Versace, Louis Vuitton, Armani etc. Be sure to have a drink in the Bamboo Bar on level 5, then choose a Japanese or international meal.

More to see Tokyo City View 1,148ft (350m) above sea level offers great views on a clear day or of sparkling lights at night. Mori Art Center, the world's first institution affiliated with the Museum of Modern Art in New York, is located on the same level and admission charges include access to this cutting-edge gallery that specializes in art, urban design and city architecture. The museum shops and the Roppongi Hills Art and Design store sell art and design products, and books from around the world.

HIGHLIGHTS

- Cutting-edge design
- Tokyo City View
- Mori Arts Center
- Public art
- Landscaped open areas
- Brand-name shops
- Variety of dining

INFORMATION

www.roppongihills.com/en

- G8; Locator map B4
- Mori Tower, 6-10-1 Roppongi, Minato-ku
- 6406–6652
- Daily 9am–1am
- Roppongi
- Good
- Free; Tokyo City View expensive
- Yebisu Garden Place (► 34), National Diet Building (► 41)

A sculpture outside the Mori Art Center

33

Yebisu Garden Place

INFORMATION

www.gardenplace.co.jp/english

✚ F10; Locator map B4

✉ 1 Mita, Meguro-ku and 4 Ebisu, Shibuya-ku

☎ General information: 5423–7111

◕ Mon–Wed, Sat–Sun 11–7, Thu–Fri 11–8; museums closed Mon. Restaurant hours vary

🍴 Beer hall, restaurants, fast-food outlets

🚇 Ebisu

🚉 Ebisu

♿ Good

🎟 Free (except Museum of Photography)

❓ Chain of moving walkways from JR Ebisu Station. Maps and signs say Ebisu for the area and station, Yebisu for the development

The old Sapporo Brewery site is one of the city's most imaginative developments—a luxury hotel, two brilliantly designed museums, a shopping complex and, from atop Yebisu Garden Palace Tower, sweeping city views.

The beer connection As a serious polluter, the red-brick brewery had to go, but the company held on to the site, moved its offices here, and created 1,000 luxury apartments. Some of the brewing equipment went into a beer museum, where it takes on the quality of sculpture. The brewing process is explained and in a virtual reality brewery tour you see what it's like to be a molecule going through fermentation. Then you get to sample a glass of the product (▶ 63).

Museum of Photography The second museum on the site, the Tokyo Metropolitan Museum of Photography (▶ 56) showcases the latest photographic techniques and displays of historic equipment. Don't miss the History of Images display in the basement.

Time out Along with the Mitsukoshi department store, there's a big restaurant complex with a huge beer hall reminiscent of a Munich *bierkeller* of the 1930s. Window-shoppers might want to check out the Glass Square complex. The Westin Tokyo Hotel is worth a visit; there's a good view from the bar or restaurant on the 22nd floor.

Above: The Museum of Photography
Right: A mash copper in
34 *the Beer Museum*

Top **25**

8

Sengakuji Temple

This temple offers an insight into Japanese values: The heroes commemorated are honored for their loyalty, single-mindedness, efficiency, ruthlessness and collective action. They lived and died by the samurai code.

Code of honor Sengakuji was one of the three great temples of Edo, and it is still one of the most important in Tokyo. After their lord Asano Takuminokami was unjustly forced into suicide in 1701, Yoshitaka Oishi and 47 loyal retainers (*ronin*, meaning "masterless *samurai*") vowed to avenge him. They raided the castle of the chief instigator, Yoshinaka Kira, beheaded him, and carried the head in triumph to Asano's tomb at Sengakuji. They in turn were required by their code to commit ritual suicide, a duty they accepted as an honor. Before killing himself, Oishi chivalrously returned Kira's head to his family. The receipt for "one head" signed by the temple priests can still be seen in the museum. The story spread quickly and has captured Japanese imaginations ever since. It has been told and retold as Kabuki (▶ 80) and puppet theater, in movies and on television.

The tombs and museum Oishi and his followers were all buried at Sengakuji. The 47 simple stones are arranged in a square, with the larger tombs of Asano and his wife, and Oishi and his son, nearby. Clouds of smoke rise from incense sticks placed in front of each tomb by the many worshipers who come to honor the dead heroes. In the museum, there are polychrome statues believed to be exact likenesses of Oishi and his son, so detailed that you can study every aspect of their dress. Their armor and weapons, including some fearsome spiked maces, are displayed separately.

HIGHLIGHTS

- Sanmon, the main gate
- Shoro, the Bell Tower
- Tombs of the 47 *ronin*
- Tombs of Asano and Oishi
- Temple gardens
- Polychrome statues of the 47 *ronin*
- *Samurai* weapons and armor
- Original clothing

INFORMATION

- H10; Locator map C4
- 2-11-1 Takanawa, Minato ku
- 3441–5560
- Daily 9–4
- Small restaurants in nearby street
- Sengakuji (exit A2 and head uphill)
- Few
- Temple free. Museum inexpensive

Above: Tombstones at Sengakuji Temple

Tokyo Tower

HIGHLIGHTS

- Observation decks at 492ft and 820ft (150m and 250m)
- General view from 820ft (250m)
- View of Mount Fuji (1 day in 5)
- Tokyo Tower Trick Art Gallery
- Aquarium
- Hologram exhibition

INFORMATION

http://www.tokyotower.co.jp

H8; Locator map D4

4-2-8 Shiba Koen (Park), Minato-ku

3433–5111

Daily 9am–10pm

Snack bars and cafés

Kamiyacho, Onarimon

Good (possible to first level)

Expensive

Zojoji Temple (➤ 37)

Tokyo's answer to the Eiffel Tower exceeds the original in height by 30ft (13m). Come on a clear day for a fine view of the Sumida River and Tokyo Bay, Ginza and the Imperial Palace.

The tower At Kamiyacho subway station, emerge from Exit 1 and head uphill. It takes about seven minutes to walk to the foot of the tower. Built in 1958 to carry television transmissions, it now broadcasts all Tokyo's channels as well as FM radio stations. Cameras at the 1,093-ft (333m) level keep an eye on the city's notorious traffic and send pictures to a central control room, which is the source of the information flashed up along the expressways. The tower is the world's tallest freestanding iron structure. The view from the 492-ft (150-m) level is not remarkable; you need to pay extra to go to 820ft (250m) where the view is good on a clear day.

The extras There is is a mixed bag of attractions around the base and lower levels, all expensive. An aquarium, on the first floor, holds 50,000 fish of some 800 varieties, and its shop sells many colorful species. On the fourth floor is the Trick Art Gallery where 3D pictures are painted in special paints to create unusual effects. The third floor has a wax museum and an exhibition of hologram technology.

Top: The view from the 1,092-ft (333-m) high Tokyo Tower
Above: Tokyo Tower by night

Zojoji Temple

Among the city's touching sights are the rows of little statues of Jizobosatsu, the protector of the souls of stillborn children. Some hold whirling toy windmills.

The temple Zojoji, the chief temple of the Jodo-Buddhist sect, was founded in 1393. It was the family temple of the Tokugawa clan, and when Ieyasu Tokugawa became *shogun* with Edo as his power base, he set about enlarging and beautifying it. The *Sanmon*, (two-storied) main gate, built in 1605 in Chinese Tang Dynasty style, is a rare example of early Edo-period architecture in Tokyo. All the other buildings at Zojoji were destroyed in 1945 and were later replaced by concrete replicas. An ancient black image of Amita Buddha is carried in procession three times a year, on January 15, May 15 and September 15.

The gardens Near the Sanmon, a cedar tree planted by President Ulysses S. Grant in 1879 also miraculously survived the 1945 air raids and fires. As at many temples, prayers written on folded paper are tied like white flowers to the smaller trees and bushes. Nearby, the outlines of two feet said to be those of Buddha are incized in a rock that was probably brought from China (like similar work in the Tokyo National Museum). Also in the garden is a large temple bell, said to have been cast in 1673 from the ornamental hairpins of court ladies. Colorful and sad at the same time are the multiple images of Jizobosatsu, or Jizo, the Buddhist equivalent of an angel, dressed in red baby bonnets. Mothers who have experienced stillbirth or who have had an abortion, may dedicate an image of the deity and decorate it with baby clothes, toys and little windmills.

HIGHLIGHTS

- Sanmon, the restored 1605 gate
- Main hall of the temple
- Great Bell of 1673, 10ft (3m) high
- Cedar tree planted by President Grant
- Stone engraving of Buddha's feet
- Gardens, flowering trees in spring
- Folded paper prayers on bushes
- Multiple images of Jizo

INFORMATION

- ✚ J8; Locator map D4
- ✉ Shiba Koen, Minato-ku. (Lies across the street below Tokyo Tower)
- 🕐 Sunrise–sunset
- Ⓜ Onarimon, Shiba-koen
- ♿ Few
- 💲 Free
- ↔ Tokyo Tower (▶ 36)

Little statues of Jizo are dressed in red baby bonnets

Imperial Palace East Garden

HIGHLIGHTS

- Otemon (gate)
- Flowering cherry trees
- Sculpted hedges
- Monumental stonework
- Base of old castle keep
- Museum of the imperial collections
- Waterbirds
- Giant carp
- Yells of martial arts students

INFORMATION

- J5; Locator map D2
- Chiyoda-ku
- Daily 9–4 (no entry after 3pm)
- Otemachi, Takebashi
- Tokyo
- Good
- Free
- Natinal Museum of Modern Art (▶ 39)
- More of Imperial Palace grounds can be seen by special permission. For information
  ☎ 3213–1111 ext 485. Tickets must be collected day before visit. Passports required. Tour times 10–11.30, 1.30–4

This was once part of the emperor's private garden. Bordered by the massive palace walls, the carefully tended gardens and their water features offer a haven for city workers from the nearby financial district.

Gateway The Imperial Palace East Garden (Higashi Gyoen) is a vast green space in the heart of the city. Once the biggest fortress in the world, the *shogun*'s castle of Edo, became the site of the Imperial Palace after 1868. The East Garden is only a fraction of the whole, but is still big enough for a long walk. The usual entrance is through the Otemon, near the Palace Hotel; it was the main castle gate, one of 36 in the outer walls, elaborately designed for defense. If you think you hear the ghosts of warring *samurai* shouting, it's probably the police martial arts class in the hall next to the guard house. A small museum near the gate shows exhibits from the imperial collections.

The sights A short walk brings you to the massive foundations of the castle keep, crowning a low hill. Notice the perfect fit of the huge stones in the walls: Mortar free, they were designed to withstand earthquakes. There's a good view over the gardens and the city from the top, but imagine the former tower here standing five stories high, and the whole hill densely packed with buildings. The tower was destroyed by fire in 1657, and most of the remaining buildings were razed after the Meiji emperor was restored to power in 1868. The gardens always offer something in bloom, notably azaleas and cherry blossom in spring and irises in summer. Huge carp thrive in the uninviting moats, and cormorants perch in wait for smaller fry.

National Museum of Modern Art

This is the place to see the best of 20th-century painting by Japanese artists, many of them influenced by the West. Here their creations are exhibited side by side with major works by their European contemporaries.

The museum The National Museum of Modern Art (Kokuritsu Kindai Bijutsukan) is in Kitanomaru Park, formerly a part of the Imperial Palace gardens. The severe concrete box of a building was designed by Yoshiro Taniguchi and built in 1969. Inside, the galleries are spacious and skillfully lit. The ground floor houses temporary exhibitions, the top three the permanent collection. Many foreign visitors are initially drawn to the familiar work of Klee and Chagall, and the fine portrait of Alma Mahler by Kokoschka; and then turn to works of Japanese painters who worked in France and Germany early in the 20th century. Tetsugoro Yorozu's nudes might almost be by Matisse, and Tsuguharu Fujita was practically an honorary Frenchman. Some of the most ravishing pictures are by those who developed the Japanese idiom in new ways—as in Kanzan Shimomura's luminous *Autumn Among Trees*, Gyokudo Kawai's 12-panel *Parting Spring*, and Shinsui Ito's *Snowy Evening*.

Crafts gallery Just across Kitanomaru Park is an impressive brick building of 1911—once headquarters of the Imperial Guard. It now houses exhibitions of 20th-century craft work, including fine textiles, graphic design, ceramics, lacquer-work and metalwork, both traditional and modern.

HIGHLIGHTS

- *Ascension*, Tatsuoki Nambata
- *Portrait of Alma Mahler*, Kokoschka
- *Deep Woods*, Keigetsu Matsubayashi
- *Bathing*, Taketaro Shinkai
- *Stream*, bronze nude by Taimu Tatahata

INFORMATION

- www.momat.go.jp/english-page/index-e
- J4; Locator map D2
- 3-1 Kitanomaru Koen, Chiyoda-ku
- 3214–2561
- Tue–Sun 10–5, (also Fri in summer until 8; closed Tue if Mon a national holiday
- Takebashi
- Good Moderate

Nude Beauty, *Tetsugoro Yorozu*

Yasukuni Shrine

HIGHLIGHTS

- Steel *torii* weighing 100 tons
- Flocks of white doves
- Japanese garden and flowering trees
- *Samurai* armor and weapons
- Carrier-borne Mitsubishi Zero
- Man-guided torpedo
- Oka, rocket plane replica
- Tributes to fallen heroes
- Historic newsreels
- War campaign timelines

INFORMATION

http://www.yasukuni.or.jp

➕ H4; Locator map C2

✉ 3-1-1 Kudankita, Chiyoda-ku

☎ Museum: 3261–8326

🕐 Shrine daily sunrise–sunset. Museum daily 9–5 (last admission 4.30); closed Jun 22–23, Dec 28–31

🍴 Café

Ⓜ Kudanshita (Exit 1)

♿ Good

🎟 Shrine free. Museum inexpensive

Japan's war dead are remembered at this most important of Shinto shrines. The adjacent War Memorial Museum, Yushukan, honors those killed in action and includes a suicide plane, military memorabilia and weaponry.

Spirits and sacrifices Yasukuni shrine on Kudan Hill, northwest of the Imperial Palace, was founded on the orders of Emperor Meiji in 1869 for the worship of the spirits, the *mitima*, of those who had sacrificed their lives in the battles for the restoration the previous year. Now it honors the 2.5 million who died "in the defense of the empire" in the years that followed, although it is controversial because these deaths mainly occurred in aggressive wars in China, the Pacific and Southeast Asia. Flocks of white doves live on the grounds of the shrine.

Instruments of destruction The museum commemorates the Russo-Japanese War of 1905, the invasion of Manchuria and World War II. Exhibits range from *samurai* armor and swords to 20th-century guns, tanks and planes, including a carrier-borne bomber and a replica Oka, a *kamikaze* rocket-powered winged bomb. Newsreels of the last days of World War II show fleets of B-29s showering bombs on Japan, *kamikaze* pilots taking off on their one-way missions, the devastation caused by the atomic bombs, and the emperor's surrender speech in August 1945.

Statue of Masujiro Ohomura near the entrance to Yasukuni Shrine

National Diet Building

This art-deco building, capped by a stepped pyramid, houses Japan's national legislature and is opulent inside. Sessions—which you can watch from the public gallery or on closed circuit TV—can be lively or tedious.

The building A competition was held in 1918 for designs for a new Imperial Diet Building (Kokkaigijido); work started in 1920 and took 16 years to finish. Japanese militarism was growing at the time, and the last thing the generals who controlled the government wanted was a genuine parliament. Many politicians then became involved in the debate over what the final building should look like and whether the building should be Japanese or Western in style and by a Japanese or a foreign architect. When the odd-looking building finally opened, the Imperial Diet had become no more than a rubber stamp. Not until 1946 was there the first general election with universal suffrage, with women finally gaining the vote. The following year the new National Diet met, replacing the old Imperial Diet.

Visits When the Diet is in session you can sit in the public gallery of either house. You need your passports and, for some sessions, a letter of introduction from your embassy. Admission is by token, which you can get at the office on the north side of the building. Riots in the Diet are not unknown, but proceedings are rarely so exciting—as you can see on the TV screen in the entrance hall. Most speakers read from prepared scripts which address contentious issues only in the vaguest of terms. When the Diet is not in session, organized tours take you into the 491-member House of Representatives, the 252-member House of Councillors (Japan's senate) and a selection of other rooms.

HIGHLIGHTS

- Marble halls and bronze doors
- House of Councillors
- Imperial throne
- House of Representatives
- Public gallery
- Stained-glass ceilings
- Emperor's Room
- Lacquer and mother-of-pearl decoration
- Avenue of gingko trees, golden in the fall

INFORMATION

www.sangiin.go.jp/eng

- ✚ H6; Locator map C3
- ⊠ Chiyoda-ku
- ☎ 5521–7445
- ◷ Mon–Fri 8–5; closed national holidays and Dec 27–Jan 3
- 🍴 Snack bar
- Ⓢ Kokkaigijido-mae, Nagatacho
- ♿ Good
- 🎫 Free
- ↔ Hie Jinja shrine (➤ 58)
- ❓ Guided tours of the building when the Diet is not in session. Carry your passport

Hibiya Park

HIGHLIGHTS

- Bonsai shops
- Ponds and fountains
- Floral borders all year
- Outdoor concerts
- Imperial Hotel, opposite
- Intricate trellises
- Hibiya City–winter skating

INFORMATION

- J6; Locator map D3
- Chiyoda-ku
- 3501–6428
- Dawn–11pm
- Good restaurant; snack bars
- Hibiya, Uchisaiwaicho
- Yurakucho
- Good
- Free
- Ginza (► 43), Idemitsu Museum of Arts (► 54)

Chrysanthemums are highly prized in Japan

In this tranquil corner of the city, Tokyo's first public park, secretaries from nearby offices eat their box lunches, lovers can find private retreats, and tired tourists rest up from sightseeing.

Six acres (2.5ha) Hibiya Park is a green extension of the Imperial Palace Outer Garden. On one side of Hibiya Park are the ministry buildings of Kasumigaseki, the edge of Ginza is only a block away on the other. In the park itself fountains play, waterbirds swim on the ponds and gardeners groom the flowerbeds and trim the trees into impeccable order. The constructions of rope and wood they build to support precious specimens through the winter snows are works of art. There are public tennis courts, a shop that sells bonsai trees, and on weekend afternoons occasional pop and rock concerts in the outdoor auditorium. Mostly though, people come to stroll and sit, away from crowds and traffic. Visitors from out of town always like to be photographed here.

The vicinity Facing the southeast side of the park is the massive Imperial Hotel (1970), which replaced Frank Lloyd Wright's 1920s original, deemed too small and too difficult to maintain and torn down in 1967. The new hotel's vast lobby is one of Tokyo's favourite meeting points. Nearby Hibiya City, an office building and shopping complex, is modeled after New York's Rockefeller Plaza, with an outdoor skating-rink in winter. Across the Harumi-dori from the Imperial Hotel is the Dai-Ichi building—once General MacArthur's headquarters.

Ginza

The Ginza neighborhood has the most expensive real estate on earth, and its stores and clubs have prices to match. On a par with New York's Fifth Avenue, you can browse elegant stores alongside Toyko's wealthiest citizens.

Stores The name Ginza derives from the silver mint that the *shogun* built in the area in 1612. Money attracts money, and merchants soon set up shops nearby. Their successors are the famous department stores of today, two of which—Wako and Mitsukoshi—stand at the heart of Ginza, the "Yon-chome" (4-chome). This is where the intersection of two main streets meet, Harumi-dori and Chuo-dori. On Sunday afternoons the latter is closed to vehicles; when the weather is fine, cafés put out tables and umbrellas. Prices are high in most stores. But not all the shopping is on a grand scale. Down the side streets, you can find boutiques and little specialty stores where prices are almost reasonable, along with hostess clubs and bars where they are outrageous. Restaurants can be extraordinarily expensive too, but you can find something sensibly priced at one of the department stores (➤ 75, panel), and side streets.

Sights Ginza's wide, straight streets date from 1872, when a fire destroyed much of the area, which covers dozens of blocks. Although many buildings today are steel-and-glass and have neon signs, several late 19th-century buildings survive, including the Wako store with a famous clock tower, which is a landmark. Down Harumi-dori near Higashi-Ginza subway station is the rebuilt Kabukiza Theater with matinée and evening performances on most days. Continue in the same direction and you will reach Tsukiji Fish Market and the Sumida River.

HIGHLIGHTS

- Ginza 4-chome crossing
- Lights of Ginza by night
- Wako's elegant displays
- People watching
- Basement food departments
- Mikimoto pearl shop
- Kabukiza Theater
- Beer halls
- Side street discount shops
- Sunday strolling on Chuo-dori

INFORMATION

- K6–K7; Locator map E3
- Chuo-ku
- 24 hours
- Countless restaurants and fast-food outlets
- Ginza, Higashi-Ginza
- Yurakucho
- Few
- Free
- Hibiya Park (➤ 42), Sony Building (➤ 44), Tsukiji Fish Market (➤ 46), Idemitsu Museum of Arts (➤ 54), Kabukiza Theater (➤ 80)

Sony Building

HIGHLIGHTS

- Super-realistic video games
- Big screen HDTV
- Tiny Walkmans and DVDs
- Minidiscs
- Digital cameras
- Global positioning
- Playstation
- Entertainment robots

INFORMATION

http://www.sonybuilding.jp

K6; Locator map D3

5-3-1 Ginza, Chuo-ku

3573–2371

Daily 11–7; closed Jan 1

Cafés on several levels; restaurants in same building

Ginza

Yurakucho

Few

Free

Ginza (➤ 43)

The Sony Plaza

Here six floors of electronic marvels, including some devices that will not have yet reached your home town, are set up for hands-on testing. There's always a queue of eager people waiting to test the latest Playstation.

Showroom Japan leads the world in consumer electronics, launching an endless succession of innovations. Sony—one of the biggest companies and the one that put "Walkman" into the world's dictionaries—is in the forefront, and this center in Ginza is its shop window. Here you can not only see new products but also try them out. If you haven't yet caught up with Super Audio CDs, Entertainment Robots, or digital cameras, this is your chance. Miniaturization is a specialty and you'll see tiny cellular phones, personal CD players, minicams and DVD recorders. Positioning equipment using earth satellites was top secret not so many years ago; now there are simple hand-held models that will tell you accurately where on earth you are and mark the spot on a map.

Demonstrations Now that everyone has a television, the industry has to produce something better and the marketing wizards have to persuade people to buy it. High definition television (HDTV) is already here; you can see its brilliantly crisp pictures on a huge screen. Check out the Air Board, a cordless, hand-held flat screen that uses wireless technology for portable viewing. Try the latest laptop computers with their built-in digital cameras and microphones that transmit your image and voice to other computers. Other tenants in the building include BMW, clothing shops, and many restaurants.

Hama Rikyu Garden

The scene at this tranquil 62-acre (25-ha) garden can have changed little since feudal lords came duck hunting here. Ponds, planted thickly with reeds and bamboo, provide cover for the hundreds of waterfowl.

The garden Now hemmed in between an expressway and the Sumida River, the Hama Rikyu Garden, also known as Hama Detached Palace Garden, was once part of the private game reserve of the Tokugawa *shogun*s and comprises water, woods and gardens. It came into the hands of the imperial family in 1871 and was given to the city in 1945. Clever planting ensures that some species are always in bloom, and big areas are much more naturalistic and wild, and less formal than in the typical Japanese garden. The river is tidal this close to its mouth, and seawater flows in and out of one of the ponds. Long causeway bridges with wisteria-covered trellises lead across the river to a replica of the picturesque Nakajima teahouse where Emperor Meiji entertained President Ulysses S Grant and Mrs. Grant in 1879. The 300-year-old pine tree near the entrance was planted by one of the early *shogun*s.

River boats Apart from the pleasure of strolling, the best reason for a visit is to catch one of the frequent water buses for a cruise upriver to the area of Asakusa, with its temple and small shops (▶ 51). Boats leave the the eastern tip of the garden every half-hour or so, for a 45-minute trip that gives you a completely different view of Tokyo. Nearby Hinoda Pier—a five-minute walk from Hamamatsucho station—is the terminus for other Tokyo Bay cruises including those to Shinagawa Aquarium (▶ 64), Odaiba (▶ 49) and bay sightseeing tours.

HIGHLIGHTS

- River views
- Duck lakes, once used for hunting
- Seawater tidal pond
- Causeway bridges
- Teahouse
- Japanese formal garden
- Peony garden
- Flowering trees, all year
- Precious trees wrapped up for winter
- River cruises

INFORMATION

- ✚ K8; Locator map D4
- ✉ 1-1 Hamarikyuteien, Chuo-ku
- ☎ 3541–0200
- 🕐 Tue–Sun 9–4.30; closed Dec 29–Jan 3
- 🚇 Shinbashi, Higashi-Ginza
- ♿ Good
- 💰 Moderate
- ↔ Tsukiji Fish Market (▶ 46)

Tsukiji Fish Market

HIGHLIGHTS

- Fish market, 5–7.30am
- Buyers checking fish
- Auctioneers and their entourage
- Sunrise over Sumida River
- The wholesale market
- Honganji Temple
- Pretty Namiyoke ("Wave Calm") Shrine
- Sushi breakfast

INFORMATION

www.tsukiji-market.or.jp/tukiji_e

➕ K7–L8; Locator map E3

✉ Tsukiji, Chuo-ku

🕐 Mon–Sat 5am–3pm, closed Sun, national holidays and market holidays (check at tourist offices)

🍴 Superb sushi bars and many noodle stalls

🚇 Tsukiji, Higashi-Ginza

💵 Free

↔ Ginza (➤ 43), Hama Rikyu Garden (➤ 45)

Even though the famed early morning tuna auctions are now not open to visitors, the world's largest fish market is still an amazing spectacle, with its mind-boggling array of fish and hive of frenetic activity.

The auctions Since the Japanese are particular about their sushi and sashimi, seafood has to reach the consumer in perfect condition. An enormous industry ensures that it does, and 90 percent of the fish eaten in Tokyo passes through Tsukiji Fish Market in the Central Wholesale Market. The action begins at 5am, when buyers inspect the giant bluefin tuna, smaller yellowfin, and aptly named "big eyes", flown in fresh from all over the world. Visitors are not permitted at the auctions, but there is still plenty to see from the sidelines as the huge tunas are wheeled away to awaiting vans.

The market In the neighboring wholesale market, 1,200 stalls sell every sort of fish and crustacean, many of them still jumping or crawling. Buyers for the city's restaurants and shops crowd the narrow alleys as struggling

masses of fish are poured from one container to another, water floods onto the floor and into the shoes of the unwary (so wear boots or tie plastic bags over your footwear) and when you've seen enough duck into one of the sushi bars (➤ 68) nearby for a Japanese breakfast.

A market trader prepares her stall in Tsukiji Fish Market

National Museum of Western Art

You may not have come to Tokyo to see masterpieces of European art, but the collection of this museum, mainly formed by one visionary in the early 20th century, is far too good to miss.

The museum The National Museum of Western Art (Kokuritsu Seiyo Bijutsukan) is on the right of the main gate to Ueno Park from the JR station. The modernist concrete building, designed by Le Corbusier, holds the art collection of Kojiro Matsukata. Matsukata was a successful businessman who spent a lot of time in Europe in the early 20th century and developed a passion for the work of the French Impressionists. His collection eventually numbered hundreds of works, including some of the finest paintings by Monet, Renoir, Gauguin (in his pre-Tahiti period) and Van Gogh, over 50 of the most famous Rodin bronzes (including *The Thinker* and *The Burghers of Calais*) and El Greco's *The Crucifixion*. Matsukata kept them in Europe, but after World War II they were brought to Japan and bequeathed to the nation in his will. The museum was opened in 1959.

The growing collection Kojiro Matsukata's inspired acquisitions are still the museum's greatest strength, but major purchases since then have filled the gaps in the collection. At one end of the time scale there are works by Old Masters, including Tintoretto, Rubens and El Greco; moderns are represented by Max Ernst, Jackson Pollock and others. You can stroll among the sculptures in the museum's courtyard; inside, good lighting does justice to the wonderful works of art. There are also some excellent traveling exhibitions.

HIGHLIGHTS

- *Crucifixion*, El Greco
- *Summer Evening Landscape in Italy*, Claude-Joseph Vernet
- *The Loving Cup*, D. G. Rossetti
- Rodin bronzes
- *Landscape of Brittany*, Gauguin
- *On the Boat*, Monet
- *Water Lilies*, Monet
- *Parisiennes in Algerian Costume*, Renoir
- *The Port of St Tropez*, Signac
- *The Petrified Forest*, Ernst

INFORMATION

www.nmwa.go.jp

- L2; Locator map E1
- 7-7 Ueno Park, Taito-ku
- 3828-5131
- Tue–Sun 9.30–5 (til 8pm Fri); closed Tue if Mon a national holiday, and Dec 26–Jan 4
- Drinks stand; snacks outside
- Ueno
- Ueno (Park exit)
- Good
- Expensive
- Tokyo National Museum (➤ 48), Shitamachi Museum (➤ 56), Ueno Zoo (➤ 64)

Above: Rodin's The Burghers of Calais *in the museum courtyard*

47

Tokyo National Museum

HIGHLIGHTS

- Jomon-era clay masks
- 3rd-century BC bronze bells
- Terracotta burial figures
- Decorative tiles
- Imari ware
- Noh costumes, 16th–18th centuries
- 1664 palanquin
- Sword collection
- Han Dynasty stone reliefs
- Tang Dynasty horses and camel

INFORMATION

www.tnm.jp
- L1; Locator map E1
- 13–19 Ueno Park, Taito-ku
- 3822-1111
- Tue–Sun 9.30–5; closed Tue if Mon a national holiday, and Dec 26–Jan 3
- A small restaurant serves snacks and light meals
- Ueno
- Ueno
- Good
- Moderate
- National Museum of Western Art (► 47), Shitamachi Museum (► 56), Ueno Zoo (► 64)

A great museum sparks your interest in fields you never thought about before. Here you can learn about every aspect of Japanese art and archeology and view a fine collection of other Asian art. Simply breathtaking.

The Japanese collection The central Honkan building displays the finest of Japanese art: not only painting and sculpture, but calligraphy, ceramics including the celebrated Imari ware, kimons, swords, armor and *ukiyo-e* (woodblock prints; ► 55, panel). There are exquisite *noh* theater costumes, some dating from the 16th century. English explanations are limited mainly to names and dates.

Archeology The Heiseikan, the newest of the five main buildings of the Tokyo National Museum (Tokyo Kokuritsu Hakubutsukan), was built in 1999 and forms a new wing to the left of the Honkan building. It houses relics found in archeological digs all over Japan: prehistoric flint axes, elaborate pottery from around 3,000BC, bronze bells and sword blades. Many intriguing terracotta burial figures—musicians, horses and wild boars—date from the 3rd to 6th centuries.

Other Asian art The Toyokan building includes exhibits of Chinese jade and bronzes, 1st-century stone reliefs, Tang Dynasty ceramic horses and a camel, precious porcelain, and textiles. Korea, Southeast Asia, Iran, Iraq and even ancient Egypt are represented. Gondara Buddhist sculpture from Central Asia shows the influence of ancient Greek art during and after the time of Alexander the Great. Be sure to look inside the Hyokeikan building, built as a memorial for the marriage of the Meiji Crown Prince in 1909.

Odaiba

A vacant stretch of reclaimed land until not long ago, this latest mega development now boasts an amazing collection of entertainment, shopping and exhibition facilities, and even its own beach.

Palette Town Complex Start at Mega Web, a hands-on museum that showcases the latest in automotive technology. Included in the complex is Future World, a glimpse at future transport with a 3D coaster ride, and a History Garage, that displays classic cars from the 1950s to the 1970s. Not far away, you can savor the bay views from the Giant Sky Wheel, the world's largest. The adjoining Sun Walk shopping complex includes restaurants and the women's mega mall, VenusFort, done in 18th-century style, sculptured fountains and artificial "sky." Check out the nearby National Museum of Emerging Science and Innovation (► 62).

Decks, Joypolis and Seaside Park Built to resemble a giant passenger liner, the Decks shopping and entertaiment complex has an array of boutiques and includes the Tokyo Joypolis, a virtual reality center with thrilling rides and video games. The man-made beach at Seaside Park is popular for sunbathing but as it is a harbor the water here is not suitable for swimming.

Mediage, Aqua City and Fuji TV Headquarters At Mediage, along with cinemas you will find the mini funparks: Where the Wild Things Are, Airtight Garage and the the Beatles' Yellow Submarine Adventure. The adjoining Aqua City retail complex has a Toys 'R' Us. Near the Daiba Station is the futuristic Fuji Television building with an observation deck, designed by architect Tange Kenzo, and opened in 1997.

HIGHLIGHTS

- Mega Web
- NeoGeo World
- Giant Sky Wheel
- History Garage
- VenusFort
- Decks Tokyo Beach
- Aqua City/Mediage
- Tokyo Joypolis
- View of Rainbow Bridge

INFORMATION

- ✚ Off map to south; Locator map F4
- ✉ Rinkai-fukutoshin
- ☎ For information:
  Mega Web 3599–0808
  VenusFort 3599–0700
  (Women's shopping; men welcome)
  Palette Town 3529–1821
  Tokyo Joypolis 5500–1801
  Aqua City 3599–4700
  Mediage 5531–7800
  Fuji TV 0180–993–188
- 🕐 Daily 10–10; some vary
- 🍴 Restaurants and cafés
- 🚃 Yurikamome line from Shimbashi Station to various stations
- 🚢 Hinode Pier to Odaiba Seaside Park
- ♿ Good to excellent
- 💰 Free to expensive
- ❓ The area is reached via the impressive Rainbow Bridge by train or it is possible to walk at a charge of ¥300.

The futuristic Fuji TV Headquarters

49

Edo-Tokyo Museum

HIGHLIGHTS

- Audiovisual hall
- Hands-on exhibits
- Middle-Jomon period dwelling
- Nihonbashi Bridge
- Earthquake display
- Reconstructed Tokyo
- Model A Ford
- Edo Castle

INFORMATION

www.edo-tokyo-museum.or.jp/english

N4; Locator map F2

1-4-1 Yokoami, Sumida-ku

3626–9974

Daily 9.30–5.30 (also Thu, Fri until 8); closed Mon and Dec 28–Jan 4

Restaurant and café

Ryogoku

Excellent

Moderate

Volunteer guide service for the permanent exhibit (in English). Films, library, good shop

This state-of-the-art museum, opened in 1993, celebrates the history and culture of Tokyo in such a dramatic and interesting way that it certainly merits the reputation as the city's premier history museum.

The building The futuristic museum was inspired by an old warehouse and rises up to 203 ft (62m), about the same height as Edo Castle's topmost tower. The museum covers Tokyo's history from the 17th century to the present.

Earthquakes and esthetics You enter the permanent exhibition space, spread over two floors, via a reproduction of a wooden Hihombashi bridge, a structure made famous from countless woodblock prints. The area beyond is divided into three sections—History Zone, Edo Zone, and Tokyo Zone—each filled with diverse displays ranging from business life, the esthetics of Edo, and urban culture and pleasure. Displays covering civilization and enlightenment are not far from those covering the two great 20th-century disasters to befall the city, the 1923 Kanto earthquake and the firebombing of Tokyo in 1945. Original material and images are included, as well as large-scale models and faithful reproductions. Special interest exhibitions and lectures are regularly held, and in the audiovisual hall there are three-dimensional images of the past. A library on Level 7 is open to the public.

An exhibit at the Edo-Tokyo Museum

50

Asakusa Kannon Temple

Old Japan lives on in the bustling Asakusa quarter. The temple ceremonies are more colorful than those elsewhere in Tokyo, and there's always a crowd here intent on shopping at the many stalls.

The people's favorite Now dedicated to uniting the competing Buddhist factions, the Asakusa Kannon Temple (Sensoji Temple) has its origins in the 7th century. Pilgrims came from all over Japan, and the Asakusa neighborhood set about entertaining them—providing food and lodging, theaters, houses of pleasure and *onsen* (baths). The area, leveled by earthquakes, bombs and fires was always rebuilt to resemble the original and remains a favorite haunt of out-of-town visitors and the foreigners who discover it. Late afternoon is a good time to come, when dozens of food stands send up tantalizing aromas and circus performers amuse the crowds.

The sights Near the subway station, opposite the Kaminarimon gate entrance to the temple grounds, is the local information center for maps and leaflets. Through the gate is Nakamise-dori, a pedestrian street lined by little shops, which leads to a second gate, Hozomon, with an elegant five-story pagoda. Straight ahead lies the main shrine hall, just beyond a great bronze urn wreathed in incense, which visitors wave over themselves in the belief that it has curative properties. To the right (west) of the temple is Asakusa Jinja, a Shinto shrine. The east gate, Nitenmon, survives largely intact from the year 1618.

A bronze Buddha in the temple gardens

HIGHLIGHTS

- Nakamise-dori: little shops
- Hozomon (gate)
- Five-story pagoda
- Worshipers "washing" in smoke
- Main Sensoji Shrine
- Tokinokane Bell
- Denbo-in Temple Garden (► 60)
- Chingodo Temple
- Rice-cracker makers
- Clowns and acrobats

INFORMATION

- ✚ N2; Locator map F1
- ✉ 2-3-1 Asakusa, Taito-ku
- ☎ 3842–0181
- 🕐 6am–sunset
- 🍴 The area is noted for good restaurants
- 🚇 Asakusa
- ♿ Good
- 🎟 Free
- ↔ Sumida River cruise (► 45), Kappabashi (► 63)
- ❓ Included in many city tours

51

Tokyo Disney Resort

HIGHLIGHTS

- Space Mountain
- Splash Mountain
- It's a Small World
- Star Tours
- "Fantillusion" evening parade
- Fireworks
- Photo opportunities
- Spectacular resort hotels

INFORMATION

www.tokyodisneyresort.
co.jp/tdr/index_e
- Off map; Locator map off F3
- 1-1 Maihama, Urayasu-shi
- 045/683–3777 (English language information)
- Open 9am; closing time varies from 7 to 10pm. Closed for six days in mid-Jan
- Many restaurants and snack bars
- Urayasu, then bus
- Maihama, (15 minutes from Tokyo Station via Keiyo Line), then free shuttle bus
- Very good Expensive
- Tour companies offer day trips from Tokyo. 40 minutes by shuttle bus from Narita International Airport, Tokyo Station (Yaesu north exit) or Ueno Station (Iriya exit)

The plummet from the summit of Splash Mountain

Since its launch in 1983 Tokyo Disneyland, modeled exactly on that in California, is as popular as ever. Now, at an adjacent site, Tokyo DisneySea features seven ports themed to the myths and legends of the sea.

Disneyland A near replica of the California original, the Tokyo version has all the most popular rides and attractions found in other Disney parks. On busy days, mainly weekends and holidays, you may have to stand in line for half an hour for Big Thunder Mountain, Space Mountain, or Star Tours.

DisneySea This consists of attractions, live entertainment, shops and restaurants in themed areas that include: Mediterranean Harbor with its Venetian gondolas; American Waterfront with a transit steamer; Port Discovery with the heart-stopping StormRider; Lost River Delta with a live performance showcasing the rainforest; Arabian Coast, which includes an Arabian Night adventure; Mermaid Lagoon, where kids can ride aboard flying cartoon fish; and Mysterious Island,

where you can explore the depths of the ocean with Captain Nemo.

Staying over The five big resort hotels, in the Tokyo Bay area clustered adjacent to the Disney Resort, are perfect for those wishing to take time to explore both parts of the Disney complex.

TOKYO's
best

Art Collections

BRIDGESTONE HIGHLIGHTS

- *Mlle Georgette Charpentier Seated,* Renoir
- *Saltimbanque Seated with Arms Crossed,* Picasso
- *Windmills on Montmartre,* Van Gogh
- *Self-portrait,* Manet
- *Mont Sainte-Victoire and Château Noir,* Cézanne
- *Still Life with Cat,* Tsuguharu Fujita
- *Faunesse,* Rodin
- Degas bronzes
- *Desire,* Maillol

BRIDGESTONE MUSEUM OF ART

The founder of the Bridgestone Tire Company used some of his wealth to buy art and opened this museum in the company's building in 1952. He specialized in the French Impressionists, Post-Impressionists and Meiji-period Japanese artists who painted in western style. A sculpture collection includes ancient Egyptian, Greek and Roman, as well as 20th-century works.

➕ L6 ✉ 1-10-1 Kyobashi, Chuo-ku (entrance on Yaesu-dori) ☎ 5777 8600 ⏰ Tue–Fri 10–8, Sat–Sun 10–6; closed late Dec to early Jan 🍴 Café nearby 🚇 Kyobashi, Nihonbashi ✋ Moderate

HARA MUSEUM OF CONTEMPORARY ART

Displays a large collection of abstract Japanese, US and European art from the 1950s to the present day. Housed in an art deco house built by art collector Hara Toshio in 1938, six galleries ranged off long corridors display perfectly the unconventional art. The additional café overlooks pleasant lawns and more outdoor art.

➕ Off map to south ✉ 4-7-25 Kita Shinagawa, Shinagawa-ku ☎ 3445–0651 ⏰ Tue–Sun 11–5 (also Wed until 8) 🍴 Café 🚇 Shinagawa ✋ Expensive

IDEMITSU MUSEUM OF ARTS

The Asian art on display here—including calligraphy, painting and ceramics is superb. Two 16th-century screens—one of cherry blossom, the other of colourful kimonos—show that Japanese reverence for these subjects is nothing new. The collection, formed by oil industry magnate Sazo Idemitsu (1885–1981), is so vast that only a tiny fraction can be shown at one time. One room is devoted to the odd but fascinating archive of pot sherds of the world. Check out the great view of central Tokyo from the museum's windows.

➕ K6 ✉ Kokusai Building 9F, 3-1-1 Marunouchi, Chiyoda-ku ☎ 5777–8600 ⏰ Tue–Sun 10–5; closed Dec 29–Jan 3 🍴 Free tea 🚇 Yurakucho ✋ Moderate

NEZU INSTITUTE OF FINE ARTS

Located in the smart area of Aoyama, the Institute is a treasury of Japanese, Chinese and Korean fine arts collected by businessman Nezu Kaichiro, who died in 1940. The gallery is in its own beautiful gardens, several with tea ceremony pavilions.

➕ F8 ✉ 6-5-1 Minami-Aoyama, Minato-ku ☎ 3400–2536 ⏰ Tue–Sun 9.30–4.30; closed day after national holidays 🍴 Café Gazebo 🚇 Omotesando (10-minute walk) ✋ Expensive

Toshusai Sharaku's Sawamura Sojuro III in the Role of Kujaku Saburo *in the Ota Memorial Museum of Art*

OTA MEMORIAL MUSEUM OF ART

At this museum you have to exchange your shoes for slippers. The *ukiyo-e* prints (see panel opposite), and the original paintings from which they were made, were collected by business magnate Seizo Ota (1893–1977). He amassed 10,000 examples, and the museum has since acquired more, so the displays are frequently rotated.

🔢 E7 ✉ 1-10-10 Jingumae, Shibuya-ku ☎ 5777–8600 ⏰ Tue–Sun 10.30–5.30; closed from 26th to end of each month and Dec 19–Jan 2 🍴 Drinks and snacks in basement 🚇 Meijijingu-mae 🚉 Harajuku JR 🖐 Moderate

A ceramic dish with a pine tree design in the collection of the Suntory Museum

SEIJI TOGO MEMORIAL ART MUSEUM

Many of the paintings on show here are by Seiji Togo (1897–1978), whose work depicts the grace and beauty of Japanese women. The museum made headlines when it paid a world-record price for Van Gogh's *Sunflowers* in 1987, and is noted for its 33 pictures by the American primitive artist, Grandma Moses.

🔢 C4 ✉ 1-26-1 Nishi-Shinjuku, Shinjuku-ku ☎ 3349–3080 ⏰ Tue–Sun 9.30–5; closed Dec 27–Jan 4 🍴 Restaurants in same building 🚇 Shinjuku 🚉 Shinjuku 🖐 Moderate

SUNTORY MUSEUM

The famous whiskey company is a great patron of the arts. This museum houses a small but beautiful display of some of the best of Japanese traditional art in rotating exhibitions of paintings, ceramics, lacquerware, textiles and carvings from the museum's own collection, or on loan.

🔢 G6 ✉ 1-2-3 Moto-Akasaka, Minato-ku ☎ 3470–1073 ⏰ Tue–Fri, Sat–Sun 10–5, (also Fri until 7) 🍴 Tea house; restaurants in same building 🚇 Akasaka-mitsuke 🖐 Moderate

TOKYO METROPOLITAN ART MUSEUM

The spacious galleries here accommodate touring exhibitions and modern art shows. There is also a small permanent collection of 20th-century Japanese art, mostly in western styles.

🔢 L1 ✉ Ueno Park, Taito-ku ☎ 3823–6921 ⏰ Tue–Sun 9–5 🍴 Café 🚇 Ueno 🖐 Free (except special exhibitions)

WATARI MUSEUM OF CONTEMPORARY ART

This small gallery specializes in cutting-edge art with new exhibitions every few months. The gift shop sells sketchbooks, photo albums, a huge selection of art postcards and arty T-shirts.

🔢 E7 ✉ 3-7-6 Jingumae, Shibuya-ku ☎ 3402–3001 ⏰ Tue–Sun 11–7 🍴 Café 🚇 Gaienmae 🖐 Expensive

UKIYO-E

Woodblock prints (*ukiyo-e*) were art for the common people, depicting views, beautiful women and Kabuki actors. They were highly popular beginning about 1700, and new designs are still being produced today. Among the greatest names, Katsushika Hokusai (1760–1849), painter of *The 36 Views of Mount Fuji*, and Utagawa Hiroshige (1797–1858) are well known internationally. Early prints in fine condition are worth fortunes, and even modern hand-colored copies can be expensive. These days, color-laser copies make a convincing substitute.

Museums

OH YOKO!

The John Lennon Museum presents an account of the life of the brilliant ex-Beatle through the somewhat biased eyes of his Japanese wife Yoko Ono. Displays, arranged chronologically, include artworks, photographs, original song manuscripts, clothes and musical instruments. His best music is featured on speakers and headphones. The poignant final room presents his words in respectful silence.

➕ Off map to north ✉ Saitama New Urban Center ☎ 048–601–0009 🕐 Wed–Mon 11–6 🍴 Nearby 🚇 Saitama Shin-Toshin on JR Keihin line 💰 Expensive

---

In the Top 25

🔲 EDO-TOKYO MUSEUM (► 50)
🔲 TOKYO NATIONAL MUSEUM (► 48)
🔲 YEBISU GARDEN PLACE (► 34)

JAPANESE SWORD MUSEUM

Gleaming and flawless, the blades kept in this museum are up to 900 years old. They are deadly weapons transmuted by age and beauty into works of art. You really can see why they were credited with magical power.

➕ C5 ✉ 4-25-10 Yoyogi, Shibuya-ku ☎ 3379–1386 🕐 Tue–Sun 9–4; closed Dec28–Jan 4 🍴 Nearby 🚇 Sangubashi 💰 Moderate

MUSEUM OF MARITIME SCIENCE

Designed to resemble a concrete ship, this museum of ships and models is sited on an island in Tokyo Bay. Historic vessels are moored nearby.

➕ Off map in Tokyo Bay ✉ 3-1 Higashi-Yashio, Shinagawa-ku ☎ 5500–1111 🕐 Mon–Fri 10–5, Sat–Sun 10–6, national holidays 10–6; closed Dec 28–Jan1 🍴 Restaurant and snack bar 🚇 Fune-no-kagakukan (from Shinbashi via Yurikamome monorail) 🚢 River bus from Hinode Pier (K8) 💰 Expensive

TOKYO METROPOLITAN MUSEUM OF PHOTOGRAPHY

The museum is part of the 1990s Yebisu Garden Place development (► 34). Early photographs on show include some from before the Meiji Restoration of 1868, recording daily life of the time. Imaginative displays demonstrate time-honored optical illusions and their modern equivalent, holography.

A gallery in the Museum of Photography

➕ E10 ✉ 1-13-3 Mita, Meguro-ku ☎ 3280–0099 🕐 Tue–Wed, Sun 10–6, Sat, Thu–Fri 10–8; closed Tue if Mon is a national holiday and 28 Dec–4 Jan 🍴 Coffee shop 🚇 Ebisu 💰 Moderate

SHITAMACHI MUSEUM

A compact museum recording working-class life of a century ago. Check out the merchant's shop, sweet shop and coppersmith's home. You can handle everyday objects and view early photographs.

➕ L2 ✉ 2-1 Ueno Koen, Taito-ku ☎ 3823–7451 🕐 Tue–Sun 9:30–4.30 🍴 Snack bar 🚇 Ueno 💰 Inexpensive

Views from the Top

AKASAKA PRINCE

The hotel stands on a central hilltop site, so the bar and restaurant on the top of its 40 stories have the city's best view of Akasaka, the Imperial Palace, Ginza and Tokyo Bay.

🏢 H6 ✉ 1-2 Kioi-cho, Chiyoda-ku ☎ 3234–1111 🕐 Daily 11.30am–midnight 🍴 Bar and restaurant 🚇 Nagatacho

KEIO PLAZA HOTEL 47TH FLOOR

The rooftop of the first skyscraper to be built in Shinjuku is a spectacular vantage point. At night, the window seats in the hotel's penthouse cocktail bars wouldn't suit sufferers from vertigo, and the prices are similarly elevated.

🏢 D4 ✉ 2-2-1 Nishi-Shinjuku, Shinjuku-ku ☎ 3344–0111 🕐 Daily 10–6 🍴 Snacks, plus many restaurants in hotel 🚇 Shinjuku 💰 Moderate

SUMITOMO TOWER

This 52-story, six-sided building with a hollow center has a lookout point, and the top three floors are given over to restaurants used by office workers for lunch, some staying open in the evening. Window tables have the kind of view you might get from a spaceship.

🏢 D4 ✉ 2-6-1 Nishi-Shinjuku, Shinjuku-ku 🕐 Daily 9am–10pm 🍴 Many restaurants 🚇 Shinjuku 💰 Free

SUNSHINE CITY OBSERVATORY

One of the world's fastest elevators carries you to the 60th floor in under a minute. Choose a clear day: When the smog is bad you can see only the local area. The same huge complex also houses the Ancient Orient Museum and a planetarium. An aquarium on the 11th floor is home to 20,000 fish of over 600 species, a coral reef, snowy penguin habitat and outdoor marine garden. The seawater for the tanks comes from Tokyo Bay.

🏢 Off map ✉ Sunshine City, 3-1-3 Higashi-Ikebukuro, Toshima-ku ☎ 3989–3331 🕐 Jul 21–Aug 31 daily 10–8.30; 1 Sep–Jul 20 Mon–Sat 10–6, Sun and national holidays 10–6.30 🍴 Restaurants and snack bars 🚇 Higashi-Ikebukuro 💰 Expensive

WESTIN TOKYO HOTEL

The 22nd-floor bar and restaurant here, and the top of Yebisu in the same complex, look out on the Yebisu Garden Place (➤ 34), north to Shibuya, and east to Shinagawa and the bay.

🏢 E10 ✉ Yebisu Garden Place, 1-4-1 Mita, Meguro-ku ☎ 5423–7000 🕐 Daily 11am–midnight 🍴 Bar and restaurant 🚇 Ebisu

An aerial view of the skyscrapers of Shinjuku

IKEBUKURO

One of Tokyo's most interesting growth areas, and easy to reach by several subway lines and JR's Yamanote loop between Shinjuku and Ueno, Ikebukuro is one of the city's liveliest places. Once a working-class district, big business has planted a few enormous buildings and the city's largest department stores, including the huge Seibu, trendy Parco and the amazing Tokyu Hands DIY store (➤ 78). Toyota's Amlux showroom (➤ 62) is across the street from Sunshine City, the multilevel women's shopping mall.

57

Shrines & Temples

SHINTO

Most Japanese are to some extent followers of Shinto, which they call *Kami-no-Michi*, meaning "the Way of the Gods (or Spirits)." Originating as a belief in the spirits of nature, it places great emphasis on purity of conduct, mind and motive, and corresponding physical cleanliness. A Shinto shrine (*jinja* or *jingu*) is marked by its *torii* gate or gates, shaped like a giant perch for the mythical cock which crowed and brought the sun goddess Amaterasu out of her cave to light up the world.

HANAZONO SHRINE

Now surrounded by the monuments of commerce and pleasure, this is one of the oldest shrines in Tokyo. People pray here for success in business.

➕ E4 ✉ Opposite Marui Interior store, Shinjuku Sanchome, Shinjuku-ku ⏱ Sunrise–9pm 🍴 Plenty nearby 🚇 Shinjuku Sanchome 👆 Free

HIE JINJA SHRINE

One of Tokyo's most picturesque shrines is opposite the main entrance to the Capitol Tokyu Hotel, up a steep flight of steps. You will notice statues of monkeys carrying their young: One of the deities enshrined here is believed to protect women against miscarriages. Hie Jinja was a favorite of the *shogun*s and the site of Edo's greatest religious festival.

➕ H6 ✉ 2-10-5 Nagatacho, Chiyoda-ku ☎ 3581–2471 ⏱ Sunrise–sunset 🚇 Kokkaigijido-mae 👆 Free

KANDA MYOJIN SHRINE

One of Tokyo's oldest foundations and the focus of the Kanda Festival, held in alternate years in May. The festival's highlight is a procession of dozens of portable shrines. The present shrine buildings are replicas of those destroyed in the earthquake and fires of 1923. On Sundays young couples come to have their weddings blessed, the brides gorgeously arrayed in their most expensive kimono.

➕ K3 ✉ 2-16-2 Soto-Kanda, Chiyoda-ku ☎ 3254–0753 ⏱ Sunrise–sunset 🚇 Ochanomizu 👆 Free

KIYOMIZU KANNON TEMPLE

Bullet holes in the Kuromon gate date from the 1868 battle for the hill. Childless women pray to a Kannon figure in the temple, and, if they subsequently have a baby, return to leave a doll in gratitude and to pray for the child's good health. Every September 25 the accumulated dolls are burned in a great bonfire.

➕ L2 ✉ Ueno Koen, Taito-ku ⏱ Sunrise–sunset 🍴 Plenty nearby 🚇 Ueno 👆 Free

SOGENJI TEMPLE

Close to the Kappabashi shops (► 63), this is also known as Kappa Temple, a name derived from the legendary water sprites who helped to drain the marshes that once covered this area.

➕ M1 ✉ 3-7-2 Matsugaya, Taito-ku ☎ 3841–2035 ⏱ Sunrise–sunset 🚇 Iriya 👆 Free

Shrine workers at Hie Jinja

SUMIYOSHI SHRINE

Fishermen were brought to this island in the Sumida River from Osaka by Ieyasu Tokugawa to set up a fishing industry. It was they who built this shrine to the god who protects them when they are at sea.

✛ M7 ✉ 1-1 Tsukuda, Chuo-ku ☎ 3531–3500
🕔 Sunrise–sunset 🚇 Tsukishima 💲 Free

TOGO SHRINE

Set amid gardens and overlooking a lake, the shrine is a tribute to Admiral Togo, Japan's naval hero in the 1905 destruction of the Russian fleet at Tsushima. Tokyo's largest antiques market is held here on the 1st, 4th and 5th Sundays of the month.

✛ E6 ✉ Off Meiji-dori, Harajuku, Shibuya-ku ☎ 3403–3591
🕔 Sunrise–sunset 🚇 Meijijingu-mae 💲 Free

TOSHOGU SHRINE

This shrine, dating from 1651, is dedicated to the first Tokugawa *shogun*, Ieyasu, who died in 1616 and was quickly proclaimed divine. One of few vestiges of the early Edo period, it somehow escaped destruction in the 1868 battle between adherents of the emperor and those of the Tokugawas, when most buildings on Ueno hill were burned down. The path from the *torii* is lined by over 200 stone and bronze lanterns.

✛ L2 ✉ 9-88 Ueno Koen, Taito-ku ☎ 3822–3455 🕔 9.30–4.30
🍴 Food stands nearby 🚉 Ueno 💲 Moderate

YUSHIMA SEIDO SHRINE

This shrine was founded in the 17th century for the study of Confucianism, not strictly a religion, more a philosophy and code of conduct. The shrine building is unusually austere. The first training institute for teachers was set up here in 1872, and in due course it evolved into Tokyo University.

✛ K3 ✉ 1-4-25 Yushima, Bunkyo-ku ☎ 3251–4606
🕔 9.30–4 🚉 Ochanomizu 💲 Free

Bronze lanterns line the path to Toshogu Shrine

SHRINE ETIQUETTE

Japanese who visit a shrine go through elaborate rituals upon entering. Tourists need only to dress respectably, although short sleeves and shorts are acceptable–use discretion. The rituals are:

● Pass under the *torii* (gate)
● Wash hands thoroughly in the stone basin
● With the dipper, pour water into a cupped hand and rinse the mouth
● Approach the shrine and throw coins into the offertory box
● Bow deeply twice
● Clap hands twice (or pull the bell rope)
● Bow once more

Parks & Gardens

The scenic Rikugien Garden

LANDSCAPE IN MINIATURE

The Korakuen garden was laid out in the 17th century by a refugee from Ming Dynasty China who scattered it with tiny replicas of famous Chinese lakes, rivers and mountains. The miniature landscape even extends to growing a small field of rice, duly harvested in October. There's a collection of bridges, ranging from simple stepping stones to the Full Moon Bridge, a half circle of stone that, with its reflection, forms a perfect O. The huge weeping cherry tree near the gate was near to dying some years ago, unable to blossom. It was saved by the botanical version of a heart transplant: New roots were grafted onto it.

DENBO-IN TEMPLE GARDEN

Entry to the lovely private garden of the temple is by ticket only (collect from the office next to the Asakusa pagoda ➤ 51). The garden is reached by the temple's side gate (facing Denboin-dori, opposite Asakusa Public Hall). It was designed in the early 17th century by the tea ceremony master Enshu Kobori. The garden pond, with resident carp and turtles, beautifully reflects the abbot's quarters and more distant pagoda.
✚ N2 ✉ Asakusa, Taito-ku ◷ Mon–Fri 10–2.30 🍴 Plenty nearby ◎ Asakusa ♿ Free

KIYOSUMI GARDEN

Across the Sumida River opposite the Tokyo City Air Terminal, this is an oddity. A pond stocked with 10,000 carp is surrounded by many and varied rocks brought from all over Japan.
✚ N5–N6 ✉ 3-3-9 Kiyosumi, Koto-ku ☎ 3641–5892 ◷ Daily 9–4.30 ◎ Morishita ♿ Moderate

KOISHIKAWA KORAKUEN GARDEN

Tokyo's oldest garden was laid out in the 17th century for one of the Tokugawa family, a relative of the *shogun*. Over the years, it was reduced to a quarter of the original size, and all the buildings—tea houses, gates and shrines—were destroyed in World War II. Now

restored, it's a sanctuary for office workers with their
lunch boxes, and housewives seeking some space.
✚ J3 ✉ 1-6-6 Koraku, Bunkyo-ku ☎ 3811–3015 🕔 Tue–Sun
9–5; closed Tue if Mon is a national holiday and Dec 29–Jan 3
🍴 Plenty nearby 🚇 Suidobashi 🎫 Moderate

NEW OTANI HOTEL GARDEN

Next to the giant hotel is a fine traditional Japanese
garden with streams and lily ponds, decorative
bridges and manicured shrubs. It continues the
tradition of an early Edo-period garden on this site.
✚ G5 ✉ 4-1 Kioi-cho, Chiyoda-ku ☎ 3265–1111 🕔 Daily 9–9
🍴 In hotel 🚇 Yotsuya 🎫 Moderate (free for hotel guests)

RIKUGIEN GARDEN

Widely regarded as the city's most beautiful Japanese
garden, Rikugien was laid out in 1695 for a patron
with literary tastes: the name means "six poem
garden," and each of its scenic features was inspired
by a poetic reference. Cloistered away from the noise
of the city by a high brick wall, this is landscaped art
of a high order, entirely artificial yet seemingly natural.
✚ Off map to north ✉ 6-16-3 Honkomagomae, Bunkyo-ku
☎ 3491–2222 🕔 Tue–Sun 9–5; closed Dec 29–Jan 3 🚇 Sengoku,
Sugamo (Toei Mita Line) 🎫 Moderate

UENO PARK

The park is the home of several museums, concert
halls and a zoo (► 64). Some of Tokyo's homeless
sleep out in the open here, even in the coldest
weather. In spring locals come in their thousands to
admire the cherry blossom. Check out
the ducks and geese on Shinobazu
Pond, where species from the Arctic
and Siberia spend the winter.
✚ L1–L2 ✉ Ueno Koen, Taito-ku 🕔 Tue–Sun
sunrise–sunset; closed Tue if Mon is a national
holiday) 🍴 Restaurants and food stands
🚇 Ueno 🚉 Ueno JR (Park exit more convenient
than subway) 🎫 Free (museums, shrines and the
zoo charge entry fees)

YOYOGI PARK

Once an imperial army training
ground, then renamed Washington Heights by the
US occupation forces who used it for housing, the
area became the site of the 1964 Olympic village and
was renamed Yoyogi Park. The park's paths, lawns
and wooded areas are pleasant to stroll through. The
Yoyogi Sports Center, just across the road, was also
created for the Games. Its stadium's pillarless roof is
still strikingly modern.
✚ D6 ✉ Yoyogi, Shibuya-ku 🕔 5am–5pm 🍴 Snacks
🚇 Meijijingu-mae, Harajuku 🎫 Free

JAPANESE GARDENS

Japanese gardens generally
come in three types, although
larger gardens can contain the
elements of more than one.
Hill gardens, with miniature
hills and a pond or stream, an
island, bridges and a
meandering path, imitate
nature and may allude to
famous beauty spots without
actually mimicking them. **Flat
gardens** have few plants:
rocks, raked gravel and sand
are designed to aid
contemplation. **Tea gardens**,
next to a tea house, have
flowing lines to contrast with
the tea house's austere
simplicity.

*The boating lake near
Ueno Park*

High-Tech Wizardry

Inside Toyota's Amlux building

MARKET LEADER

Since the 1960s, Japan has been first in the field of consumer electronics, almost monopolizing every new invention—color TV, digital cameras, video recorders, microwave ovens, mobile phones, personal computers—for a few years while high profits can be made. Then, as the rest of the world catches up and prices fall, lower-cost manufacturers in Korea, Taiwan and China, Malaysia and Thailand take over while Japan moves on to the next amazing product.

In the Top 25

🔳 **METROPOLITAN GOVERNMENT OFFICES (► 28)**

🔳 **SONY BUILDING (► 44)**

FUJITA VENTÉ

The latest electronic and video games, including virtual reality, can be tried out here. The building is also a venue for art and architecture exhibitions.

➕ D5 ✉ Fujita Building BF, 1F and 2F, 4-6-15 Sendagaya, Shibuya-ku ☎ 3796–2486 🕐 Fri–Wed 10–6; closed Dec 26–Jan 3 🍴 Snacks 🚉 Yoyogi 🎫 Free (except special exhibitions)

NATIONAL MUSEUM OF EMERGING SCIENCE AND INNOVATION

Seven floors of the very latest scientific technology dispayed with hands-on exhibits as well as events that provides an opportunity to meet scientists. Themes include the environment and technological change, and a dome theater presents issues on a spherical screen.

➕ Off map to south ✉ 2-41-3 Aomi, Koto-ku ☎ 3570–9151 🕐 Tue–Sun 10–5 🚉 Fune-no-Kagakukan (on Yurikamome line) 🎫 Moderate

NEC SHOWROOM

This is a hands-on exhibition of current model computers and communications technology.

➕ J6 ✉ C Plaza, Hibiya Kokusai Building B1F, Hibiya City, 2-2-3 Uchisaiwaicho, Chiyoda-ku ☎ 3595–0511 🕐 Mon–Fri 10–6; closed national holidays 🚉 Uchisaiwaicho 🎫 Free

NTT INTERCOMMUNICATION CENTER

Science and art converge in this exhibition and interactive display of computer graphics. The "cave" filled with modifiable 3D imagery is most spectacular.

➕ C4 ✉ Tokyo Opera City Tower 4F, 3-20-2 Nishi-Shinjuku, Shinjuku-ku ☎ 0120–144199 (toll-free) 🕐 Tue–Sun 10–6 🍴 Restaurants 53F, 54F 🚉 Hatsudai 🎫 Moderate

TEPCO ELECTRIC ENERGY MUSEUM

This museum run by the Tokyo Electric Power Company has seven floors of interactive exhibits.

➕ D7 ✉ 1-12-10 Jinnan, Shibuya-ku ☎ 3477–1191 🕐 Thu–Tue 10–6 🚉 Shibuya 🎫 Free

TOYOTA AUTO SALON AMLUX

In this futuristic blue steel and glass tower, you can climb into every car currently produced by Toyota, inspect the winners of famous Formula 1 races and learn about the latest technical wizardry.

➕ Off map ✉ 3-3-5 Higashi-Ikebukuro, Toshima-ku ☎ 5391–5900 🕐 Tue–Sat 11–7; closed Tue if Mon is a national holiday 🍴 Restaurant and snack bar 🚉 Higashi-Ikebukuro 🚉 Ikebukuro (7-minute walk) 🎫 Free

What's Free

In the Top 25

24 ASAKUSA KANNON TEMPLE (► 51)
16 GINZA (► 43)
5 HARAJUKU (► 32)
11 IMPERIAL PALACE EAST GARDEN (► 38)
4 MEIJI JINGU SHRINE (► 31)
1 METROPOLITAN GOVERNMENT OFFICES (► 28)
19 TSUKIJI FISH MARKET (► 46)

BEER MUSEUM

This is part of Yebisu Garden Place (► 34), reached by moving walkways from Ebisu JR Station. The Sapporo brewery here closed down; today you see the brewing process via virtual reality headsets. The museum's collection of advertising posters includes a gauze-clad beauty of 1908, showing that sex as an aid to sales is no new idea.

➕ E10 ✉ 4-20-1 Ebisu, Shibuya-ku ☎ 5423–7255 🕐 Tue–Sun 10–6; closed Mon and Dec 28–Jan 4 🍴 Huge beer hall, restaurants, and fast-food outlets 🚉 Ebisu 💰 Free

KAPPABASHI

What Tsukiji is to fish, Kappabashi is to plates, pans, chopsticks, knives, lanterns, signs and everything the massive restaurant business needs except food—the shops here sell only the plastic variety. A huge head crowned with a chef's hat stands on top of a tall building to mark the beginning of Kappabashi-dori.

➕ M2 ✉ Kappabashi-dori, Taito-ku 🕐 Shops: Mon–Sat 9.30–6.30; some hours vary 🍴 Wide choice 🚉 Tawaramachi 💰 Free

MEGURO PARASITOLOGICAL MUSEUM

The world's only museum of human and animal parasites. The highlight is an 26-ft (7.9-m) tapeworm.

➕ Off map ✉ 4-1-1 Shimo-Meguro, Meguro-ku ☎ 3716–1264 🕐 Tue–Sun 10–5 🚉 Meguro 💰 Free

ORIGAMI KAIKAN

You can watch work going on in the factory and demonstrations of *origami*, the art of paper folding. Special papers and paper crafts are sold in the shop.

➕ K3 ✉ 1-7-14 Yushima, Bunkyo-ku ☎ 3811–4025 🕐 Mon–Sat 9–5; closed national holidays 🍴 Snacks nearby 🚉 Ochanomizu (5-minute walk) 💰 Free

SUMO MUSEUM

A store of records, relics and pictures of past *yokozuna*—the grand masters of *sumo* wrestling—is housed in the building which is also the main venue for matches. You may see some of today's big men arriving in their stretch limousines.

➕ N4 ✉ 1-3-28 Yokoami, Sumida-ku ☎ 3622–0366 🕐 Mon–Fri 10–4.30; closed during tournaments, except to ticket holders 🍴 Snacks 🚉 Ryogoku 💰 Free

---

MODEL MENUS

Japan's famous food replicas are much appreciated by every visitor who can't speak Japanese or read a menu. The models, *sampuru*, were first devised in the 19th century to show what new foods introduced from abroad looked like, and before plastic they were made of painted plaster and gelatine. Shopkeepers were surprised when foreigners wanted to buy them, but soon adapted to the market opportunity. Realistic replicas are not cheap—a plate of plastic noodles can cost a lot more than the real thing.

Advertising posters in the Beer Museum

For Children

TOSHIMA-EN

This elaborate amusement park in a northwestern suburb has some of the wildest roller-coaster rides, loops, corkscrews and spins anywhere, including a long freefall. There are also plenty of gentler rides to suit smaller children as well as a waterpark with several pools and slides.
➕ Off map ✉ 3-25-1 Koyama, Nerima-ku ☎ 3990–3131 🕐 Wed–Mon 10–5 🍴 Snacks and fast food 🚇 Toshima-en (Seibu-Ikebukuro Line) ✋ Expensive

HANAYASHIKI

This amusement park was founded in 1853. The rides, intended primarily for children, include carousels, dodgems and a haunted house.
➕ N2 ✉ 2-28-1 Asakusa, Taito-ku ☎ 5400–6900 🕐 Wed–Mon 10–6 (also Tue during school holidays) 🍴 Snacks 🚇 Asakusa ✋ Expensive

NHK BROADCASTING CENTER

NHK runs tours of the sets used for their TV programs. Performances are in Japanese.
➕ D7 ✉ 2-2-1 Jinnan, Shibuya-ku ☎ 5400 6900 🕐 Tue–Sun 10–6; closed Tue if Mon is a national holiday 🍴 Snacks 🚇 Meijijingu-mae 🚇 Shibuya ✋ Moderate

SHINAGAWA AQUARIUM

A well-stocked aquarium with a walk-through glass tunnel, so you can feel surrounded by sharks. Shows by performing sea lions and dolphins run four or five times daily.
➕ Off map ✉ 3-2-1 Katsushima, Shinagawa-ku ☎ 3762–3431 🕐 Wed–Mon 10–5; closed Dec 29–Jan 1 🍴 Snacks 🚇 Omorikaigan (Keihin-Kyuko Line from Shinagawa) ✋ Expensive

TOKYO DOME CITY

This attraction has a giant roller-coaster, the Ultra Twister and loop-the-loop train, as well as gentler rides for younger children. The entry ticket does not include the cost of rides.
➕ J3 ✉ 1-3-61 Korakuen, Bunkyo-ku ☎ 5800–9999 🕐 Daily 10–6 🍴 Snack bars and food stands 🚇 Korakuen, Suidobashi 🚇 Suidobashi ✋ Expensive

TSUKUDA TOY MUSEUM

Tokyo's best toy museum displays a collection of over 8,000 post-Meji era toys.
➕ N2 ✉ 1-36-10 Hashiba, Asakusa ☎ 3874–5133 🕐 Wed–Sun 9.30–5 🍴 Nearby 🚇 Asakusa ✋ Inexpensive

UENO ZOO

Japan's first zoo, which opened in Ueno Park in the late 19th century, displays over 350 species including the popular giant pandas, which are fed daily at 3.30; they're not on view on a Friday. There is an open-air section where children can stroke the animals.
➕ L1 ✉ Ueno Park ☎ 3828–5171 🕐 Tue–Sun 9.30–5 🍴 Café 🚇 Ueno JR ✋ Moderate

Young visitors can view the underwater acrobatics of Shinagawa Aquarium's sealife from a glass tunnel

TOKYO
where to...

EAT

SHOP

BE ENTERTAINED

STAY

Japanese Restaurants

PRICES

Price guides for Japanese restaurants (► 66–68) are for set menus, known as *"setto,"* most restaurants offer a choice of these. Lunch sets generally cost much less than dinner.

¥   up to ¥3,000
¥¥ ¥3,000–¥8,000
¥¥¥ over ¥8,000

CHOICES

Bento: Box lunch.
Kaiseki ryori: Refined cuisine of many small delicacies, using typically Japanese ingredients.
Kushiage: Deep-fried morsels on sticks.
Miso: Soybean paste.
Ramen: Chinese noodles, in soups, usually with pork.
Robatayaki: Food cooked over a charcoal grill.
Shabu-shabu: Thin slices of beef swirled in a boiling broth, then dipped in sauces.
Soba: Buckwheat noodles.
Sukiyaki: Thinly sliced beef cooked at the table with vegetables and *tofu*.
Teishoku: Fixed-price menu.
Tempura: Shrimps, fish and vegetables coated in light batter and deep fried.
Teppanyaki: Fish, meat and vegetables cooked on a griddle.
Udon: Wheat-flour noodles.
Yakitori: Small pieces of chicken, liver or other meat, grilled on bamboo skewers.

AKA (¥¥)

A great place for post-function snacks since this late-opening bar/restaurant serves tasty fusion hors d'oeuvre. Meal menu features Okinawan dishes including tofu specialties.
🚹 N2 ✉ 2-14-3 Nagatacho, Tokyu Plaza, Akasaka
☎ 5157–0909 🕐 Mon–Sat lunch, dinner 🚇 Akasaka

BOTAN (¥¥¥)

Traditional-style dining on bamboo mats. Famous for its chicken sukiyaki that simmers before you on a charcoal brazier.
🚹 K4 ✉ 1-15 Kana-Sudacho, Kanda ☎ 3251–0577
🕐 Mon–Sat 11–9
🚇 Awajicho

FUTABA (¥)

Ueno is known especially for *tonkatsu*, fried pork cutlet, eaten with rice, soup and pickled vegetables; this is one of the oldest restaurants serving it.
🚹 L2 ✉ 2-8-11 Ueno, Taito-ku ☎ 3835–2672
🕐 Daily 11.30–2.30, 5–7.30
🚇 Ueno

HACHIUTA (¥¥)

Delicious tofu, stir-fry and selected neo-Japanese dishes are all prepared with the freshest of ingredients. You will find a selection of French and Italian wines. English is spoken here.
🚹 D8 ✉ 38-3 Udagawacho, Shibuya ☎ 3496–8009
🕐 Daily 7am–11pm
🚇 Shibuya

HASSAN (¥¥)

A busy traditional restaurant with a choice of seating on chairs or on *tatami* (straw mats). The set tempura, sukiyaki and *shabu-shabu* menus include all-you-can-eat options, at a higher price.
🚹 G8 ✉ Denki Building B1F, 6-1-20 Roppongi, Minato-ku
☎ 3403–8333
🕐 Daily 11.30–2, 5–11
🚇 Roppongi

HAYASHI (¥¥)

Kimono-clad women oversee the *hibachi* cooking operations.
🚹 D4 ✉ Hide Building, 2-22-5 Kabuiki-cho, Shinjuku
☎ 3209–5672 🕐 Mon–Sat 5–11.30 🚇 Shinjuku

KUREMUTSU (¥¥)

The specialties in this traditional house with a delightful courtyard, are grilled fish, sashimi and *kaiseki* meals. Perfect for real Japanese food but reservations essential.
🚹 N2 ✉ 2-2-13 Asakusa Walk, Nakamise ☎ 3842–0906
🕐 Fri–Wed 4–9.30
🚇 Asakusa

MAISEN (¥)

Located in a converted bath-house, diners come here for the house special *tonkatsu* (deep-fried pork cutlets). Miso soup, rice and cabbage are included in the set dishes.
🚹 E7 ✉ 4-8-6 Jingu-mae, Shibuya-ku ☎ 3470–0071
🕐 Mon–Sat lunch, dinner
🚇 Omotesando

MUNAKATA (¥¥)

Try the cheaper lunchtime meals at this intimate and popular *kaiseki* (haute cuisine) restaurant. Good boxed lunches.
🚹 K7 ✉ Mitsui Urban Hotel basement, 8-6-15 Ginza, Chou-ku

☎ 3574–9356 ⏰ Daily 11.30–4, 5–10 🚇 Shinbashi or Hibiya

MYOKO (¥)

The house specialty is *hoto* (wide, flat *udon*). Try the hot *hoto nabe* with miso broth and vegetables.
✚ D8 ✉ Shinto Building 1F, 1-17-2 Shibuya, Shibuya-ku ☎ 3499–3450 ⏰ Daily 11–9.30 🚇 Shibuya

NAKASE (¥¥¥)

A famous and long-established tempura restaurant near Nakamise-dori. Follow your nose and be prepared to wait. Often a line forms well before opening time. Lunch is best—for economy and because the area shuts down early in the evening.
✚ N2 ✉ 1-39-13 Asakusa, Taito-ku ☎ 3841–4015 ⏰ Wed–Mon noon–8 🚇 Asakusa

NAMIKI YABU SOBA (¥)

A branch of the renowned Yabu Soba, this affordable eatery specializes in tempura *soba* dishes.
✚ N2 ✉ 2-11-9 Kaminarimon, Asakusa ☎ 3841–1340 ⏰ Daily lunch, dinner 🚇 Asakusa

NOBU (¥¥¥)

Nobu Matsuhisa started as a sushi chef in Tokyo before striking out for Peru, Argentina and the US. Reservations are essential at this classy restaurant where friendly waiters serve contemporary Japanese cuisine with efficiency. Sushi and sashimi on the menu (and the sushi rolls are renowned). Or try the spicy sour shrimp or the black cod with miso.
✚ E8 ✉ 6-10-17 Minami-Aoyama, Minato-ku ☎ 5467–0022 ⏰ Mon–Fri 11.30–2, daily 6–10 🚇 Shibuya or Omotesando

SHABU ZEN (¥¥)

A big restaurant specializing in *shabu-shabu*, and including all-you-can-eat deals. Take note that the American beef is less costly than the local.
✚ G8 ✉ Three Stars Mansion, 5-17-16 Roppongi, Minato-ku ☎ 3585–5388 ⏰ Daily 5pm–11.30pm 🚇 Roppongi

Also at:
✚ K7 ✉ Ginza Core Building, 5-8-20 Ginza, Chuo-ku 🚇 Higashi-Ginza

SHINJUKU NEGISHI (¥)

Tasty country-style beef dishes are served at this popular rustic, little budget eatery
✚ D4 ✉ 2-45-2 Kabuki-cho, Shinjuku-ku ☎ 3232–8020 ⏰ Daily 11–10.30 🚇 Shinjuku

TSUNAHACHI (¥)

Fine tempura at a surprisingly fair price, but stick to the set menus.
✚ D4 ✉ 3-31-8 Shinjuku, Shinjuku-ku ☎ 3352–1012 ⏰ Daily 11–10 🚇 Shinjuku-Sanchome

YABU SOBA (¥)

One of Tokyo's most famous *soba* shops, located in an old Japanese house, decked with *shoji* screens and woodblock prints. It is so popular you may have quite a wait to get served.
✚ K4 ✉ 2-10 Kanda-Awajicho, Chiyoda-ku ☎ 3251–0287 ⏰ Daily 11.30–7.30 🚇 Awajicho

ETIQUETTE

After wiping your fingers on the moist towel (*oshibori*) brought before your meal, roll it up and keep it for use as a napkin.

Drink soup from the bowl as if it were a cup. Pick out solid pieces with chopsticks. Slurping soup and noodles is considered acceptable and normal.

To eat rice hold the bowl close to your mouth and use chopsticks.

Don't point with chopsticks, or lick the ends, or put the ends that go in your mouth into a communal dish. Don't leave chopsticks crossed or standing upright in a bowl.

If you can't manage something with chopsticks, ask for a knife (*naifu*), fork (*foku*) or spoon (*supun*).

Never blow your nose in a restaurant. Find somewhere to hide first.

Pour drinks for your companions; leave it to them to pour yours. When they do, it's polite to hold your glass up to be filled.

Sushi & Sashimi

NOT EXACTLY RAW FISH

Among Westerners, plenty of fallacies exist on the subject of sushi and sashimi. "It's raw fish, right?" Not exactly. Morsels of raw fish, shellfish and roes, as well as a few cooked varieties, pressed on to a pad of warm, vinegared rice–that's sushi (or more precisely, *nigirizushi*). Pieces of fish and vegetable rolled in rice and seaweed are *makizushi*. Delicate slices of raw fish and shellfish served with *daikon* (shredded white radish), *wasabi* (green horseradish paste) and soy sauce–that's sashimi, often served as a first course. Sushi can cost from ¥320 a selection to ¥2,400 (and even much more). If prices are not listed, ask–or you may face a shock when you receive the bill. The majority of sushi restaurants serve alchohol.

BIKKURI SHUSHI (¥)

Patrons help themselves to sushi and sashami from a sushi "train." The price varies according to dish color.

⊕ G7 ⊠ 3-14-9 Roppongi, Minato-ku ☎ 3403–1489
⊙ Daily lunch, dinner
⊜ Roppongi

EDOGIN (¥¥)

Well established and popular, offering large servings of sashimi and made from the freshest fish from the famous market nearby. Until just before they're served, the fish are still swimming in a large tank in the center of the room. Considering the freshness the prices are reasonable.

⊕ K7 ⊠ 4-5-1 Tsukiji, Chuo-ku ☎ 3543–4401
⊙ Daily 11–9 ⊜ Tsukiji

FUKUZUSHI (¥¥¥)

Not your usual sushi bar. A chic setting for great sushi in one of the liveliest night-time areas downtown. This is the up-market, expensive end of eating sushi. Unlike most sushi restaurants, this one has a cocktail bar.

⊕ G7 ⊠ 5-7-8 Roppongi, Minato-ku ☎ 3402–4116
⊙ Mon–Sat 11.30–2, 5.30–11
⊜ Roppongi

HEIROKUZUSHI (¥)

A fast-service sushi bar where food is set out on a conveyor belt in front of the counter. Just help yoiuself to your favorites, move along the line and pay at the end.

⊕ E7 ⊠ 5-8-5 Omotesando, Jingumae ☎ 3498–3968
⊙ Daily 11–9
⊜ Meijijingu-mae

KAKIYA SUSHI (¥)

This stylish restaurant serves excellent, high-quality sushi.

⊕ E7 ⊠ 1-14-27 Jingumae, Shibuya-ku ☎ 3423–1400
⊙ Daily 11–10.30
⊜ Higashi-Ginza

KYUBEI (¥¥¥)

Founded many years ago, and still going strong, Kyubei specializes in some of the most expertly made sushi around.

⊕ K7 ⊠ 8-7-6 Ginza, Chuo-ku ☎ 3571–6523
⊙ Mon–Sat 11.30–2, 5–10
⊜ Higashi-Ginza

SUSHI DAI (¥¥)

Try the *setto*, a set sushi course with tuna, eel, shrimps and other morsels, plus rolls of tuna and rice in seaweed.

⊕ L7 ⊠ Tsukiji Fish Market, Tsukiji ☎ 3542–1111
⊙ Mon–Sat 5am–2am
⊜ Tsukiji

SUSHI-SEI (¥¥)

This packed lunchtime favorite, frequented by local offices workers, offers deleicious sushi and sashami.

⊕ H6 ⊠ 3-11-4 Akasaka, Akasaka ☎ 3582–9503
⊙ Daily lunch, dinner
⊜ Akasaka

TAKENO (¥)

Located near the central fish market, this restaurant serves good-sized helpings of sushi, sashimi and tempura. A good place to go after a look around the market.

⊕ K7 ⊠ 6-21-2 Tsukiji, Chuo-ku ☎ 3541–8698
⊙ Mon–Sat 7am –2pm; closed market and national holidays
⊜ Tsukiji

Italian

CAPRICCIOSA (¥)

A cheerful place that serves large portions of pasta and other Mediterranean favorites at fair prices. One of a chain with several branches.

G7 ⊠ 7-13-2 Roppongi, Minato-ku ☎ 5410–6061 ⏰ Daily 11–11 ☻ Roppongi

CARMINE (¥)

A small, friendly establishment with carefully prepared Tuscan-style antipasto, penne and house specialties. Reservations are essential.

G3 ⊠ 1-19 Saikumachi, Shinjuku-ku ☎ 3260–5066 ⏰ Daily 11.30–2, 6–9.30 ☻ Kagurazaka

CARMINE EDOCHIANO (¥¥)

Italy meets Japan— Tuscan cuisine in a genteel old Japanese house. The setting alone makes it worth a visit.

F5 ⊠ 9-13 Arakicho, Shinjuku-ku ☎ 3225–6767 ⏰ Daily 11.30–2, 6–9.30 ☻ Yotsuya-sanchome

IL BACARO (¥)

This bar/restaurant serves tasty Italian "tapas" with a selection of good wines. The regular menu features a variety of pasta dishes.

D4 ⊠ 3-4-8 Saison Plaza BIF, Shinjuku ☎ 5269–8528 ⏰ Daily 11–10 ☻ Shinjuku

IL BOCCALONE (¥¥¥)

A north Italian-style trattoria, with good antipasti and grills and notable desserts.

E9 ⊠ 1-15-9 Ebisu, Shibuya-ku ☎ 3449–1430 ⏰ Mon–Sat 5.30–11 ☻ Ebisu

LA BOHÈME (¥)

Various pastas and sauces, pizzas, salads and ice-creams. With its late opening it is popular with night owls.

E7 ⊠ Jubilee Plaza B1F, 5-8-5 Jingumae, Shibuya-ku ☎ 5467–5666 ⏰ Daily 11.30am–4pm ☻ Omotesando

LA VERDE (¥)

Part of a chain, all of which are noted for their large servings of pasta with tasty toppings at low prices. The wines are also good and not expensive.

F6 ⊠ Aoyama Building B1F, 1-2-3 Kita-Aoyama, Minato-ku ☎ 3404–0712 ⏰ Daily 11–9 ☻ Aoyama-itchome

ROSSO E NERO (¥¥)

A good choice if you want a change from traditional Japanese fare. Here you will find home cooking, with good antipasti, a wide choice of pastas, sauces and grills. The menu includes some filling Austrian fare as well as Italian dishes, notably the fruit strudel and dumpling desserts.

G5 ⊠ Kioi-cho Building 2F, 3-12 Kioi-cho, Chiyoda-ku ☎ 3237–5888 ⏰ Daily 11.30–2, 5.30–11 ☻ Nagatacho

SICILIA (¥)

Popular for pasta, pizza and garden salads, especially on Fridays and Saturdays when you can join the loyal patrons lining up.

G7 ⊠ 6-1-26 Roppongi, Minato-ku ☎ 3305–3653 ⏰ Daily lunch, dinner ☻ Roppongi

PRICES

The prices given for non-Japanese restaurants (➤ 69–73) are for an average meal (starter and main course, or main course and dessert) per head, including service but excluding drinks.

¥   up to ¥3,000
¥¥   ¥3,000–¥8,000
¥¥¥ over ¥8,000

LINTARO (££)

Lintaro Mizuhama is the friendly owner of the restaurant that bears his name, and he is often to be found chatting with diners or directing the service. He's a Ginza native and expert: His family has been here for centuries. The deep basement room is a surprise, with its high ceiling and Renaissance pictures. The food is Italian but with Japanese notes in its presentation and flavors. The superbly fresh salads and vegetables are from the restaurant's special gardens.

K7 ⊠ 5-9-15 Ginza, Chuo-ku ☎ 3571–2037 ⏰ Daily 11–2.30, 5–11; closed New Year holiday ☻ Ginza

Indian & Sri Lankan

TOMOCA (££)

This is an agreeable, relaxed Sri Lankan restaurant where you select your curry, choosing from shrimp, fish, chicken or beef, and specify the degree of spiciness. (Don't ask for the hottest unless your digestive tract is made from cast-iron.) A whole range of extras comes with it: poppadums, salads, fried eggplant, dal and tangy *sambals*.

✚ E4 ✉ 1-7-27 Yotsuya, Shinjuku-ku ☎ 3353–7945 🕐 Daily 11–10.30 🚇 Shinjukugyoen-mae

AJANTA KOJIMACHI (¥)

An old favorite, with the simplest of settings but one of the most comprehensive menus in Tokyo. The southern and northern Indian dishes are as authentic as you will find.

✚ G5 ✉ 3-11 Nibancho, Chiyoda-ku ☎ 3264–4255 🕐 Daily 24 hours 🚇 Kojimachi

ATHARA PETARA (¥)

Classic Sri Lankan fare, including spicy chicken curry with yellow rice and vegetables. Good vegetarian selection.

✚ G7 ✉ Ryudochu Building 2F, 7-4-4 Roppongi ☎ 3478–3898 🕐 Daily 11.30am–5am 🚇 Nogizaka

ASHOKA (¥¥)

In a rather luxurious setting overlooking Chuo-dori, Ginza's main street, Ashoka serves curries and tasty tandoori-cooked chicken. Freshly made yogurt desserts are a specialty.

✚ K7 ✉ Pearl Building 2F, 7-9-18 Ginza, Chuo-ku ☎ 3572–2377 🕐 Daily 11.30–9.30 🚇 Higashi-Ginza

BINDI (¥)

Tiny counter-style eatery serving home-style Indian food. Delicious onion *pakoda* (onion rings), and *brinjals* (deep-fried eggplant). The 16 different curries provide plenty of choice.

✚ E7 ✉ 7-10-10 Minami Aoyama, Minato-ku ☎ 3409–7114 🕐 Daily 11.30–2, 6–10 🚇 Omotesando

DARJEELING (¥)

The chef here performs in front of the diners, serving chicken and vegetable curries in intimate surroundings.

✚ Off map to north of Yanaka ✉ 3-10-3 Nippori, Negishi ☎ 5685–0267 🕐 Daily lunch, dinner 🚇 Nippori

KENBOKKE (¥)

The interior here is modern with few Indian touches, but cuisine of the Bombay-born chef is authentic. Tandoori shirmp and chicken are specialties.

✚ F8 ✉ Empire Building 2F, 4-11-28 Nishi-Azabu, Minato-ku ☎ 3498–7080 🕐 Mon–Sat 11.30–10.30 🚇 Hiroo

MOTI (¥)

An old favorite of locals and expatriates alike. Standard Indian interior and menu, with tasty vegetarian dishes, *kormas* and chicken *masala*. One of five branches (others include Roppongi).

✚ H7 ✉ Kinpa Building 3F, 2-14-31 Akasaka, Minato-ku ☎ 3584–6640 🕐 Daily 11.30–11 🚇 Akasaka

PALETTE (¥)

A plain café where Sri Lankan chefs make the curries as hot as you choose, or as mild. Breads and desserts are excellent.

✚ E9 ✉ 1-15-2 Ebisu-Nishi, Shibuya-ku ☎ 5489–0770 🕐 Mon–Sat 11.30–10.30 🚇 Ebisu

TANDOOR (¥)

Good range of spicy meat and vegetarian curries. The surroundings may be basic but the service is friendly.

✚ E9 ✉ 1-9-3 Ebisu-Nishi, Shibuya-ku ☎ 3461–6181 🕐 Daily 11–10 🚇 Ebisu

Thai

BAN THAI (¥)

One of the city's oldest Thai restaurants, with a huge selection of dishes including delicious spicy warm salads. The curries are especially good.

➕ D4 ✉ 1-23-14 Kabuki-cho, East Shinjuku ☎ 3207–0068 🕐 Mon–Fri 11.30–3, 5–11; Sat–Sun and hols 11.30–11 🚉 Shinjuku

CAY (¥¥)

The Japanese-style Thai food at this trendy restaurant includes curries, salads, fried meats and noodles. Live music some nights.

➕ E7 ✉ Spiral Building 5-6-23 Minami-Aoyama, Omotesando ☎ 3498–5790 🕐 Mon–Sat 6–midnight 🚉 Omotesando

CHIANG MAI (¥¥)

Customers are crammed into two small rooms to savor the standard dishes, cooked by two Thai chefs. Try the *tom yam gung* shrimp soup, and the spicy chicken.

➕ K6 ✉ 1-6-10 Yurakucho, Chiyoda-ku ☎ 3580–0456 🕐 Daily 11–11 🚉 Hibiya

CORIANDER (¥)

The modern Thai cuisine at this ambient late-night restaurant has all the classic Thai flavors.

➕ G8 ✉ 1-10-6 Nishi-Azabu, Minatoku-ku ☎ 3475–5720 🕐 Daily 6pm–3am 🚉 Azabu-Juban

MAI-THAI (¥¥)

This is a small, cheerful, popular spot in a side street, serving a typical Thai menu at reasonable prices. One of a growing number of eating places in the fast-developing Ebisu.

➕ E9 ✉ 1-18-16 Ebisu, Shibuya-ku ☎ 3280–1155 🕐 Daily 5.30–10 🚉 Ebisu

RICE TERRACE (¥¥)

A relaxed setting for some of Tokyo's best Thai food. Service is friendly but polished. Try to get a table downstairs: The upper level is cramped. Good selection of Australian wines.

➕ F8 ✉ 2-7-9 Nishi-Azabu, Minato-ku ☎ 3498–6271 🕐 Mon–Sat 11.30–2, 6–10 🚉 Nogizaka

MEKONG (¥)

Traditional Thai fare from most regions. Try the red curry with duck or the spicy fried pork.

➕ Off map to north ✉ 3-26-5 Nishi-Ikebukuro, Toshima-ku ☎ 3988–5688 🕐 Mon–Sat 11–10 🚉 Ikebukuro

SIAM (¥¥)

A cut above the rest in Shinjuku's Kabukicho district, this restaurant specializes in northern Thai cooking. Intriguing spice combinations make the long menu, explained in English, quite an adventure.

➕ D4 ✉ Umemura Building 2F, 1-3-11 Kabukicho, Shinjuku-ku ☎ 3205–6600 🕐 Daily 5am–3am 🚉 Shinjuku

THE SIAM (¥)

This one has been around for years and is still serving tasty Thai food at prices that are economical—for Ginza—especially at lunchtime.

➕ K7 ✉ World Town Building 8F, 5-8-17 Ginza, Chuo-ku ☎ 3572–4101 🕐 Daily 11.30–2, 5.30–9.30 🚉 Higashi-Ginza

CHANG-PLAI (££)

Easily reached by the Hibya Line from Ginza, and just a short walk up the hill from the west exit of Ebisu Station, Chang-Plai is a Bangkok-style café that features a large menu of tasty street-stand style fare. The adventurous chef is creative with his special dishes. The atmosphere is casual and friendly and prices are very reasonable.

➕ E9 ✉ 1-14-15 Ebisu-Minami, Shibuya-ku ☎ 3715–4588 🕐 Daily 5–10.30 🚉 Ebisu

Other International Fare

FUSION FOOD

Californian and Australian chefs devised Pacific Rim cuisine by adding Asian ingredients to traditional European preparations. A similar process in reverse has produced a crop of restaurants in Tokyo where the dishes are western with a local twist, including Hiroyuki Masud's Bistro de Maido (¥¥), an informal restaurant in a Shibuyu basement that's popular with young business people. Salads topped with lightly salted seafoods are a specialty.

➕ D7 ✉ Miyagi Building B1, 1-10-12 Shibuya, Shibuyu-ku ☎ 3407–5724 🕔 Daily 5.30–11.30pm; closed 31 Dec–4 Jan 🚇 Shibuya

ASENA (¥¥)

Authentic Turkish *meze* (hors d'oeuvres), kebabs and much more, with a belly-dance show every Friday and Saturday.

➕ H6 ✉ Gojuban Building B1, 5-5-11 Akasaka, Minato-ku ☎ 3505–5282 🕔 Mon–Sat 5–11 🚇 Akasaka

BENGAWAN SOLO (¥¥)

Indonesian furnishings, staff and cooking. The colorful *rijsttafel*, including some highly spiced items, gives you a chance to experience the widest variety.

➕ G7 ✉ Kanako Building 1F, 7-18-13 Roppongi, Minato-ku ☎ 3408–5698 🕔 Daily 11.30–3, 5–9 🚇 Roppongi

BOUGAINVILLEA (¥¥)

Vietnamese food may yet challenge Thai in Tokyo. This place has a wide choice of authentic dishes, including noodle soups, crab with coriander, spring rolls, sweet-and-sour pork or chicken and meatballs.

➕ D8 ✉ Romanee Building 2F, 2-25-9 Dogenzaka, Shibuya-ku ☎ 3496–5537 🕔 Daily 5–11 🚇 Shibuya

EL CASTELLANO (¥¥)

An informal and high-spirited Spanish establishment with a variety of tapas, tortillas and wonderful paella. This is one of the few restaurants in Japan to serve rabbit.

➕ E7 ✉ 2-9-12 Shibuya, Omotesando ☎ 3407–7197 🕔 Mon–Sat 6–10 🚇 Shibuya

MOMINOKI HOUSE (¥)

A unique restaurant with a large contemporary Japanese–French menu. Live music on Saturday nights.

➕ E7 ✉ 2-18-5 Jingumae, Harajuku North ☎ 3405–9144 🕔 Mon–Sat 11–10 🚇 Meijijingu-mae

OMIYA (¥¥)

This French restaurant, in traditional Asakusa, has tasty beef dishes and a great choice of interesting wines.

➕ N2 ✉ 2-1-3 Asakusa, Asakusa ☎ 3844–0038 🕔 Daily lunch, dinner 🚇 Tobu Asakusa

ROSITA (¥)

Guacamole, tacos, enchiladas, chili con carne and other Mexican basics. The ambience is very folksy.

➕ D4 ✉ Pegas-Kan Building B1, 3-31-5 Shinjuku, Shinjuku-ku ☎ 3356–7538 🕔 Daily 11.30–2.30, 5.30–11 🚇 Shinjuku-san-chome

SAMOVAR (¥¥)

Authentic Russian stews and soups, kebabs, rye bread. Plenty of beers and vodkas.

➕ D8 ✉ 2-22-5 Dogenzaka, Shibuya-ku ☎ 3462–0648 🕔 Mon–Sat 5–11 🚇 Shibuya

TOKAI-EN (¥)

An enormous Korean operation, with all-you-can-eat bargain lunches. Nine floors of Korean home cooking—spicy seafood, stews and *bulgogi* barbecues are specialties. It can get boisterous in late evening.

➕ D4 ✉ 1-6-3 Kabukicho, Shinjuku-ku ☎ 3200–2934 🕔 Daily 11am–4am 🚇 Shinjuku

Burgers, Diners & Delis

ANDERSEN (¥)

A self-serve deli and sandwich bar located in the basement of a bakery. Continental or full breakfasts available.
⊞ E7 ⊠ 5-1-26 Aoyama, Minami-Aoyama
☎ 3407–4833 🕐 Daily 9–9
🚇 Omotesando

DOLE FRUIT CAFÉ (¥)

Fresh fruits and vegetables come as juices, and in tasty combinations in curries and pizzas. Many vegetarian dishes.
⊞ D8 ⊠ Kokusai Building A-Kan 2F, 13-16 Udagawa-cho, Shibuya-ku ☎ 3464–6030
🕐 Daily 11–10 🚇 Shibuya

GOOD HONEST GRUB (¥)

A friendly place for brunch. Fresh fruit and vegetable juices plus vegetarian dishes.
⊞ E9 ⊠ 1-11-11 Ebisu-Minami, Shibuya-ku
☎ 3710–0400 🕐 Mon–Fri 11.30–11, Sat–Sun, national holidays 8.30–4.30pm, dinner until 11pm 🚇 Ebisu

HARVESTER (£)

A good variety of fresh western foods including salads and pasta.
⊞ D7 ⊠ 1-13-13 Omotesando, Jingumae
☎ 3478–1031 🕐 Daily 8am–10.30pm 🚇 Harajuku JR

HOMEWORKS (¥)

Above-average hamburgers with all the extras, plus salads, snacks and sandwiches at above fast-food prices.
⊞ F9 ⊠ Shichiseisha Building 1F, 5-1-20 Hiroo, Shibuya-ku
☎ 3444–4560 🕐 Mon–Sat 11–9, Sun and holidays 11–6
🚇 Hiroo

JOHNNY ROCKETS (¥)

Good hamburgers, french fries, salads and other fast-food staples.
⊞ G7 ⊠ Coco Roppongi Building 2F, 3-11-10 Roppongi, Minato-ku ☎ 3423–1955
🕐 Sun–Thu 11–11, Fri–Sat 11am–6am 🚇 Roppongi

KUA'AINA (¥)

Well-known for its huge Hawaiian hamburgers and sandwiches.
⊞ E7 ⊠ 5-10-21 Minami-Aoyama, Minato-ku
☎ 3407–8001 🕐 Mon–Sat 11am–11.30pm, Sun and hols 11–10.30 🚇 Omotesando

NEWS DELI (¥)

New York-inspired deli fare—salads, soups, sandwiches, pastas and grills. Counter and tables, and take-out service.
⊞ E7 ⊠ SJ Building 1F, 3-6-23 Kita-Aoyama, Minato-ku
☎ 3407–1715 🕐 Daily 9am–12.30am 🚇 Omotesando

NEW YORK GRILL (¥¥)

Enjoy steak and seafood with great views from the 52nd floor of the Park Hyatt. Sunday brunch is popular so reserve ahead.
⊞ E4 ⊠ 3-7-1 Nishi-Shinjuku, Shinjuku-ku ☎ 5323–3458
🕐 Daily 11.30–2.30, 5.30–10.30 🚇 Shinjuku

TOKYO JOES (¥¥)

Come here for volume and value. The most popular dish is the butter and mustard stone crab. These crabs are flown in fresh from Florida Keys, their unique habitat.
⊞ H6 ⊠ Akasaka Eight-One Building, B1, 2-13-5 Nagata-cho. Chiyoda-ku ☎ 3508–0325
🕐 Daily 11.30–3, 5–11.30
🚇 Akasaka-mitsuke

SOUNDS FAMILIAR

The Japanese have adapted the words as they've adopted the food:
hot dog: *hotto doggu*
hamburger: *hambaga*
sandwich: *sando-ichi*
steak: *suteki*
ham: *hamu*
sausage: *soseji*
salad: *sarada*
bread: *pan*
butter: *bata*
coffee: *kohi*
bacon and egg: *bekon eggu*
orange juice: *orenji jusu*
ice cream: *aisu kurimu*
chocolate cake: *chokoreto keiki*

Shopping Districts

PRICE OF PARADISE

The shops are a pleasure to visit, the range and quality of goods outstanding, the displays beautiful, the service usually impeccable. The customer is always right. Your most mundane purchase will be wrapped as though it were a jewel beyond price. Inflation has been low for decades and, with most foreign currencies increasing in value compared with the yen in recent years, prices are much more reasonable than they used to be.

Many shops open every day, typical hours being 10–6 or 10–8. There's always some sort of promotion. Any excuse will do for a sales push, especially a holiday or festival. Purchases over ¥10,000 for export will be free of sales tax (carry your passport).

AKIHABARA

For electrical and electronic equipment. At the JR station, look for signs to Electric Town, on the west side, where seven- and eight-story buildings are stuffed with appliances
🚇 L3 🚊 Akihabara 🚉 Akihabara

ASAKUSA

Nakamise-dori, near the temple, is a street of traditional little shops several a wide range of goods.
🚇 N2 🚊 Asakusa

GINZA-YURAKUCHO

For the famous department stores on Chuo-dori and in Yurakucho, and specialist shops, craft shops and antiques shops, from Ginza 4-chome through 7-chome.
🚇 K6–K7 🚊 Ginza, Higashi-Ginza 🚉 Yurakucho

JINGUMAE-HARAJUKU

Takeshita-dori for youth fashions and fads; Omotesando-dori for higher fashion and higher prices.
🚇 E7 🚊 Meijijingu-mae, Omotesando 🚉 Harajuku

KANDA-JINBOCHO

An area with many second-hand bookshops stocking Japanese and foreign books and woodblock prints.
🚇 J4 🚊 Jinbocho

MINAMI-AOYAMA

Antiques shops along and around Kotto-dori; fashion stores on Aoyama-dori and Omotesando-dori.
🚇 F6–F7 🚊 Omotesando

SHIBUYA

For department stores, fashion boutiques, bookstores and home improvement stores.
🚇 D8 🚊 🚉 Shibuya

SHINJUKU

You'll find camera and audiovisual equipment stores west and east of the station; department stores above and east of the station.
🚇 D4–E4 🚉 Shinjuku 🚊 Shinjuku, Shinjuku-sanchome

SHIODOME

Toyko's futuristic, urban shopping, entertainment and dining precinct includes dozens of brand-name shops, great restaurants and the Nihon TV headquarters. Nearby is Tokyo Tower (► 36), Zojoji Temple (► 37) and piers that are departure points for Tokyo Bay cruises.
🚇 J8 🚉 Shimbashi

UENO

The Ameyoko market (short for Ameya Yokocho) is packed with stalls selling food, household goods and clothes, under the elevated tracks from Ueno to Okachimachi JR Station.
🚇 L2 🚊 Ueno, Ueno-Hirokoji

Department Stores

The *depato* is a Japanese institution. Visit at least one of the big ones to experience the phenomenon. The layout of the stores is easy to understand, they take credit cards, they can produce someone who speaks English, they stock almost everything, they are close to stations (they may own a line or two) and they open at weekends—big days for shopping. The weekly closing day varies from store to store.

ISETAN
An enormous store above Shinjuku-sanchome station, with dozens of designer boutiques. The food hall and restaurants are in the basement. Good deals for visitors.
➕ D4 ✉ 3-14-1 Shinjuku, Shinjuku-ku ☎ 3225–2514 🕐 Thu–Tue 10–7 🚇 Shinjuku 🚉 Shinjuku-sanchome

MATSUYA
Bright, colorful and favored by younger customers. The basement food hall sells excellent boxed meals at sensible prices.
➕ K6 ✉ 3-6-1 Ginza, Chuo-ku ☎ 3567–1211 🕐 Mon–Wed, Fri 10–6, Sat–Sun and national holidays 10–6.30 🚉 Ginza

MITSUKOSHI
Founded in the 17th century, with selections of toys, stationery, kimonos, sportswear and a fine food hall. It even has its own subway station.
➕ L5 ✉ 1-4-1 Nihonbashi-Muromachi, Chuo-ku ☎ 3241–3311 🕐 Tue–Sat 10–6, Sun and holidays 10–6.30 🚉 Mitsukoshi-mae

ODAKYU
Above part of Shinjuku Station, with its own railroad line. Food is in the lower basement, the 12th floor has an art gallery, and restaurants are on the 15th floor and top floor.
➕ D4 ✉ 1-1-3 Nishi-Shinjuku, Shinjuku-ku ☎ 3342–1111 🕐 Wed–Mon 10–7 🚉 Shinjuku

SEIBU
With adjoining Parco fashion store and theater complex. Designer boutiques, children's wear, stationery. Top-floor restaurants. Other branches in Ikebukuro and Yurakucho.
➕ D8 ✉ 21-1 Udagawa-cho, Shibuya-ku ☎ 3462–0111 🕐 Thu–Tue 10–8.30 🚉 Shibuya

TAKASHIMAYA
The basement food hall has Fauchon and Fortnum & Mason counters. Elegant displays and opulent surroundings, immaculately turned-out staff and boutiques with famous-name fashions.
➕ L5 ✉ 2-4-1 Nihonbashi, Chuo-ku ☎ 3211–4111 🕐 Thu–Tue 10–7 🚉 Nihonbashi
Also at:
➕ D4 ✉ Times Square (south of the station) 🚉 Shinjuku

TOKYU
The latest fashions for its mostly younger customers. The basement food hall is up there with the best
➕ D8 ✉ 2-24 Dogenzaka, Shibuya ☎ 3477–3111 🕐 Daily 10–8 🚉 Shibuya

IN-STORE FOOD

Department stores are a boon to visitors, and not only when they want to shop or to use the toilet facilities. Most stores have a whole selection of reasonably priced restaurants offering different food styles, normally on the top floor. But in the basement their food-to-go departments are an eye-opener, and an education in the ingredients of Japanese cuisine. The artistically prepared box lunches (*bento*) are a comparative bargain, and—if your budget is really restricted—you can taste all sorts of free samples, although they are more likely to sharpen your appetite than satisfy it.

Crafts & Souvenirs

CRAFTS

BINGO YA

Folk art, crafts, traditional toys and gifts from all parts of Japan.
➕ F3 ✉ 10-6 Wakamatsu-cho, Shinjuku-ku
☎ 3202–8778 🕐 Thu–Sun 10–7 🚇 Akebonobashi (15-minute walk)

INTERNATIONAL ARCADE

Thirty shops selling crafts and souvenirs, from the superb to the average. Several pearl shops.
➕ J6 ✉ 1-7-23 Uchisaiwaicho, Chiyoda-ku
🕐 Daily 11–9 🚇 Hibiya

ORIENTAL BAZAAR

Four levels of handicrafts, souvenirs, antiques, bric-a-brac, dolls and kimonos. Also at Narita airport.
➕ H3, M13 ✉ 5-9-13 Jingumae, Shibuya-ku
☎ 3400–3933 🕐 Fri–Wed 9.30–6.30 🚇 Omotesando

DOLLS

KYUGETSU

An established shop, selling traditional and many other dolls, in wood, papier mâché and fabric.
➕ M4 ✉ 1-20-4 Yanagibashi, Taito-ku ☎ 3861–5511
🕐 Daily 9.15–6
🚇 Asakusabashi

CERAMICS

KISSO

Fine ceramics combine traditional methods with modern designs. Shares premises with a restaurant.
➕ G7 ✉ Axis Building B1F, 5-17-1, Roppongi, Minato-ku
☎ 3582–4191 🕐 Daily 11.30–2, 5.30–9 🚇 Roppongi

KORANSHA

Fine pieces, especially the flower and bird patterns from Arita in Kyushu.
➕ K7 ✉ 5-12-12 Ginza, Chuo-ku ☎ 3543–0951
🕐 Mon–Sat 9.30–6.30
🚇 Higashi-Ginza

PAPER ART

KYUKYODO

Beautiful handmade papers and everything needed for calligraphy.
➕ K7 ✉ 5-7-4 Ginza, Chuo-ku ☎ 3571–4429
🕐 Daily 10–6 🚇 Ginza

WASHIKOBO

Washi and *mingei* (folkcraft) items.
➕ G7 ✉ 1-8-10 Nishi-Azabu, Minato-ku ☎ 3405–1841
🕐 Mon–Sat 10–6
🚇 Roppongi

ORIGAMI KAIKAN
(► 63)

FOR CHILDREN

KIDDYLAND

Sells the toys, alarm clocks and kitsch that childhood dreams are made of. A great place to shop for offbeat souvenirs. Several branches throughout the city.
➕ E7 ✉ 6-1-9 Jingumae, Shibuya-ku ☎ 3409–3431
🕐 Daily 10–8 🚇 Harajuku
🚇 Meijijingu-mae

POKEMON MUSEUM

The Pocket Monsters game and cartoon series have spun off a whole world of little creatures, and all are available here.
➕ L5 ✉ Kawasaki Teitoku Building 1F, 3-2-5 Nihonbashi, Chuo-ku ☎ 5200–0707
🕐 Daily 11–8 🚇 Nihonbashi

EVERYDAY QUALITY

If the price of fine porcelain and lacquerware comes as a shock, look instead at the everyday versions sold in street markets and department stores. The Japanese sense of colour and form extends to these too, and quality is usually faultless. Even the disposable baskets and boxes used for take-away meals can be minor craftworks. Special handmade and decorative papers, in the form of wrappings, stationery, boxes, dolls, fans and *origami* designs make good gifts—light, unbreakable and reasonably priced. The Ota Memorial Museum of Art (► 55) has an excellent shop (downstairs near the front desk) selling many paper products.

Antiques, Ornaments & Junk

FUJI-TORII

Established in 1948, this reputable dealer carries quality antiques and works of art.

➕ E7 ✉ 6-1-10 Jingumae, Shibuya-ku ☎ 3400–2777 🕐 Wed–Mon 11–6 🚇 Meijijingu-mae

HASEBE-YA ANTIQUES

An eclectic stock of pottery, bronze statuary, *netsuke*, lacquerware, and woodware—boxes, carvings and furniture.

➕ G8 ✉ 1-5-24 Azabujuban, Minato-ku ☎ 3401–9998 🕐 Mon–Sat 10.30–6 🚇 Roppongi

KAMON ANTIQUES

For oriental fine art and folk art, calligraphy and Imari ware.

➕ E8 ✉ 4-3-12 Shibuya, Shibuya-ku ☎ 3406–1765 🕐 Mon–Sat 10.30–7 🚇 Shibuya

KUROFUNE ANTIQUES

A colorful shop, well-stocked with fine porcelain, old prints, lacquerware, furniture and folk art.

➕ G7 ✉ 7-7-4 Roppongi B1F, Minato-ku ☎ 3479–1552 🕐 Mon–Sat 10–6 🚇 Roppongi

FLEA MARKETS

Sales of used goods and junk were traditionally held outside the gates of temples and shrines, and some still are. There's a tradition of settling debts before the New Year, and some people find it necessary to sell their possessions. Harder times have now made it more respectable to buy secondhand goods. Real bargains are rare, and dealers will normally have latched on to them almost before the market opens. Even so, it pays to get to the market early, as the dealers are laying out their wares. The markets are an unusual chance to bargain. Listings magazines (➤ 92) give details of upcoming sales. Regular sites and days include:

AOYAMA OVAL PLAZA

➕ E7 ✉ Near National Children's Castle, Jingumae 5-chome, Shibuya-ku 🕐 Every 3rd Sat of month 6—sunset 🚇 Omotesando

HANAZONO SHRINE

➕ E4 ✉ Opposite Marui Interior store, Shinjuku-sanchome 🕐 Every Sun 7–6 🚇 Shinjuku, Shinjuku-sanchome

NOGI SHRINE

➕ G7 ✉ Roppongi, Minato-ku 🕐 Every 2nd Sun of month 7–6 🚇 Nogizaka

ROI BUILDING

➕ G7 ✉ In front of Roi Building, Roppongi 5-chome, Minato-ku 🕐 Every 4th Thu and Fri of month 7–6 🚇 Roppongi

TOGO SHRINE

➕ E7 ✉ Harajuku, Shibuya-ku 🕐 Every 1st, 4th and 5th Sun of month 4am–2pm 🚇 Meijijingu-mae

TOKYO ANTIQUE HALL

Twenty small antiques stalls gathered under one roof. About five minutes' walk south of the Ikebukuro east exit.

➕ Off map to north ✉ 3-9-5 Minami-Ikebukuro, Toshima-ku ☎ 3980–8228 🕐 Mon–Sat 10–6 🚇 Ikebukuro

COLLECTIBLE 'ANTIQUES'

Antiques (which in Japan are anything more than about 50 years old), are generally expensive. Fine pieces fetch enormous sums, although the market has settled down since the 1980s' boom. Specifically, Japanese collectibles include ceramics, dolls, swords, lacquerware, masks, *netsuke*– a small and often intricately carved toggle of ivory or wood, used to fasten a small container to a kimono sash– paintings, woodcarvings and woodblock prints (➤ 55, panel).

Miscellaneous Stores

HIGH FASHION

The elegant young OL (► 13) in search of the latest designs patrols the fashion boutiques, conveniently clustered in "vertical malls." You can see her in action at:

La Forêt
➕ E7 ✉ 1-11-16 Jingumae, Shibuya-ku ☎ 3472–0411
🕐 Daily 10:30–7
Ⓜ Meijijingu-mae

From 1st Building
➕ F7 ✉ 5-3-10 Minami-Aoyama, Minato-ku 🕐 Daily 10.30–7 Ⓜ Omotesando

BARGAINS GALORE

Tokyo's best discount store, Don Quijote, has six levels of clothing, electricals, CDs and DVDs, souvenirs and food. Worth visiting just to view the variety of Japanese goods on offer. Tax free on purchases over ¥10,000.
➕ G7 ✉ 3-14-10 Roppongi, Minato-ku ☎ 5786-0811
🕐 Daily 11–7 Ⓜ Roppongi

BOOKS

AOYAMA BOOK CENTER
Check this one out for the large stock of American and European titles.
➕ G7 ✉ 6-1-20 Roppongi, Minato-ku ☎ 3479–0479
🕐 Daily 10–5.30am
Ⓜ Roppongi

Also at:
➕ F9 ✉ Hiroo Garden Plaza, 4-1-29 Minami-Azabu, Minato-ku
Ⓜ Hiroo

ISSEIDO
For secondhand books, art books and woodblock prints.
➕ J4 ✉ 1-7 Kanda-Jinbocho, Chiyoda-ku ☎ 3292–0071
🕐 Daily 10–7 Ⓜ Jinbocho

KINOKUNIYA
Close to the south exit of Shinjuku Station. The large stock of foreign books is located on the 7th floor.
➕ D5 ✉ Annex Building, Times Square, 5-24-2 Sendagaya, Shibuya-ku ☎ 3463–3241
🕐 Daily 10–7 Ⓜ Shinjuku

MARUZEN
Imported books, travel books and others about every aspect of Japanese life. Good for woodblock prints.
➕ L5 ✉ 2-3-10 Nihonbashi, Chuo-ku ☎ 3272–7211
🕐 Mon–Sat 10–7
Ⓜ Nihonbashi

Also at:
➕ D8 ✉ Bunkamura B1F, 2-24-1 Dogenzaka, Shibuya-ku

OHYA-SHOBO
Among several second hand book and print shops clustered along the road heading east from the station, this one has a vast stock of antique illustrated books and fine prints.
➕ J4 ✉ 1-1 Kanda-Jinbocho, Chiyoda-ku ☎ 3291–0062
🕐 Daily 10–7 Ⓜ Jinbocho

HOBBIES

TOKYU HANDS
Everything you may need for model-making, sewing, carpentry and much more.
➕ D8 ✉ 12-18 Udagawa-cho, Shibuya-ku ☎ 5489–5111
🕐 Daily 10–7 Ⓜ Shibuya

Also at:
➕ D5 ✉ Times Square, near Shinjuku Station Ⓜ Shinjuku

STATIONERY

ITO-YA
Stationery, wrapping paper, and greeting cards —Japanese and imported. Art supplies and ingenious desk accessories.
➕ K6 ✉ 2-7-15 Ginza, Chuo-ku ☎ 3561–6361 🕐 Daily 10.30–7 Ⓜ Ginza

PEARLS

MIKIMOTO
This is the big name, in the field of cultured pearls, with top prices.
➕ K6 ✉ 4-5-5 Ginza, Chuo-ku ☎ 3535–4611 🕐 Thu–Tue 10–6 Ⓜ Ginza

TASAKI PEARL GALLERY
This shop has several showrooms, and offers tours and demonstrations. City tour buses often include this on their itinerary.
➕ H7 ✉ 1-3-3 Akasaka, Minato-ku ☎ 5561–8880
🕐 Daily 9–6 Ⓜ Akasaka

Cameras & Electronics

Don't expect any real bargains. Prices may be higher than in your home country, even for Japanese-made products, although this depends on exchange rates. But it is still fascinating to see the range on offer in Japan and the local marketing methods. Tell the sales staff where you are from, so that you get the right specification of equipment: Japanese electronic shops cater to all markets.

LAOX

This giant electrical retailer has four buildings in Akihabara—the main one looks like a huge VCR standing on end. The duty-free branch is nearby at 1-13-3 Soto-Kanda. Also toys and pearls.
✚ L3 ✉ 1-2-9 Soto-Kanda, Chiyoda-ku ☎ 3253–7111 🕐 Mon–Sat 10–7.45, Sun 10–7.15 🚇 Akihabara

MINAMI MUSEN

Five floors are packed with electrical equipment, a surprising 7th floor with imported furniture, including antiques.
✚ L3 ✉ 4-3-3 Soto-Kanda, Chiyoda-ku ☎ 3255-3730 🕐 Daily 9–5.30 🚇 Akihabara

YAMAGIWA

This store, one of the biggest retailers in Akihabara, specializes in lighting fixtures and sells everything from light bulbs to satellite dishes, You'll find both domestic and imported lines.
✚ L3 ✉ 4-1-1 Soto-Kanda, Chiyoda-ku ☎ 3253–2111 🕐 Sun–Thu 10–5.30; Fri–Sat 10–8 🚇 Akihabara

PHOTOGRAPHIC EQUIPMENT

New means expensive, but since the Japanese photographer must have the latest, there is a lot of secondhand gear available at sensible prices.

SAKURAYA

Not only cameras and film, but video equipment and electronics galore.
✚ D4 ✉ 3-26-10 Shinjuku, Shinjuku-ku ☎ 3352–4711 🕐 Daily 10–8 🚇 Shinjuku

YODOBASHI CAMERA

Near the west exit of Shinjuku Station. A glitzy, multilevel, noisy, crowded store full of every sort of equipment and film. There's a branch east of the station.
✚ D4 ✉ 1-11-1 Nishi-Shinjuku, Shinjuku-ku ☎ 3346–1010 🕐 Daily 9.30–9.30 🚇 Shinjuku

MUSIC TAPES & CDS

HMV

This store has tens of thousands of CDs, casettes and videos in stock. The dozens of listening stations are often not enough for the huge crowds.
✚ D8 ✉ 24-1 Udagawa-cho, Shibuya ☎ 5458–3411 🕐 Daily 10–10 🚇 Shibuya

TOWER RECORDS

One of the world's biggest music retailers, with eight floors stocking every style of recorded music. Popular with locals.
✚ D7 ✉ 1-22-14 Jinnan, Shibuya-ku ☎ 3496-3661 🕐 Daily 10–10 🚇 Shibuya

AKIHABARA

Several blocks of multistory emporia are stuffed with everything from electronic marvels to workaday washing machines. Smaller stores specialize in computer software, mobile phones, speaker systems and even humble switches and cables. Goods flow out on to the street; sound systems are playing at pain threshhold. A lot of signs are in English. Carry your passport to benefit from duty-free concessions, and ask for discounts on any pretext you can think of.

Japanese Theater & Arts

KABUKI

The Kabuki-za Theater is a Ginza landmark, with its big hanging lanterns and posters. Full programs last four to five hours, including two intermissions; tickets cost upwards of ¥3,000 (¥13,000 for good seats). You can rent an English-language "Earphone Guide," synchronized to the action and an English program is invaluable. You can opt for a one-act play, up to 90 minutes long, for about ¥1,000 for a non-reservable, distant fifth-floor seat for which you must stand in line for 30 minutes before the show.

KABUKI-ZA THEATER
✚ K7 ✉ 4-12-15 Ginza, Chuo-ku ☎ 3541–3131
🚇 Higashi-Ginza

NATIONAL THEATER (KOKORITSU GEJIKO)
✚ H5 ✉ 4-1 Hayabusa-cho, Chiyoda-ku ☎ 3265–7411
🚇 Hanzomon

NOH

Much older than Kabuki, infinitely stylized, and performed by masked actors, *noh* is less accessible still to foreigners. Even the Japanese confess to wishing it didn't go on so long, and so slowly. The younger generation says "*Noh*? No!" Listings magazines (➤ 92) will tell you about the open-air, torch-lit performances at temples, where even the uninitiated can enjoy the gorgeous costumes and setting. A regular indoor venue is:

KANZE NOH-GAKUDO
✚ D8 ✉ 1-16-4 Shoto, Shibuya-ku ☎ 3469–5241
🚇 Shibuya

BUNRAKU

In this form of theater, three puppeteers work near-lifesize figures, while narrators tell the stories to a musical accompaniment. The stories told are similar to Kabuki and the scripts traditional and usually well known by the audience. Like *noh*, it is an esoteric art for which few foreigners acquire a taste. Performances are sometimes staged at the small hall of the National Theater (see above).

BONSAI

By carefully pruning roots and branches, a tree sapling can be kept to a miniature scale while reaching maturity. The aim is to produce a tree that looks natural in every way, except size. Some prized specimens, gnarled and apparently windswept, have been handed down for over 200 years. Check out:
Takagi Bonsai Museum
✚ G4 ✉ 1-1 Goban-cho, Chiyoda-ku ☎ 3221–0006
🕐 Tue–Sun 10–7
🚉 Ichigaya JR

IKEBANA

The art of flower arranging developed in parallel with the tea ceremony to decorate the room in a simple but exquisite fashion. The Tourist Information Center (➤ 92) can tell you about classes.

PEOPLE'S THEATER

Kabuki developed under the Tokugawa *shoguns*, and two prohibitions gave it the character is still has today. In 1629, women were banned from the stage, resulting in the tradition of *onnagata*—male actors specializing in female roles. Then it was forbidden to attend the plays wearing swords. The *samurai* class, who wouldn't be seen in public without a sword, stayed away, and Kabuki became an entertainment for the masses. The plays blend historical romance, tragedy and comedy, music, dance and acrobatics, performed in vivid costumes and make-up.

Music & Movies

CLASSICAL MUSIC

Japanese soloists and conductors have taken the world by storm, and standards of performance in Tokyo are excellent. Many foreign soloists, orchestras and opera companies also appear. Ticket prices are high (¥4,000–¥25,000). Among the many concert halls are:

BUNKAMURA ORCHARD HALL

Part of an impressive cultural center, with a theater and cinemas.
➕ D8 ✉ 2-24-1 Dogenzaka, Shibuya-ku ☎ 3477–9111
🚇 Shibuya

SUNTORY HALL

A fine new concert hall in the Ark Hills development.
➕ H7 ✉ 1-13-1 Akasaka, Minato-ku ☎ 3584–9999
🚇 Tameike-sanno

TOKYO METROPOLITAN FESTIVAL HALL

Located at the entrance to Ueno Park. Seats 2,300 in the main hall, 700 in a smaller auditorium. A small shop in the foyer sells sheet music and souvenirs.
➕ L2 ✉ 5-45 Ueno Koen, Taito-ku ☎ 3828–2111
🚇 Ueno

TOKYO OPERA CITY

Despite its name, this new theater and art gallery complex presents a varied orchestral concert program.
➕ C4 ✉ 3-20-2 Nishi-Shinjuku, Shinjuku-ku ☎ 5353–0770 🚇 Hatsudai

JAZZ

Many local and touring musicians appear in Roppongi and Harajuku clubs. Blue Note Tokyo seems to draw the biggest visiting names, but ticket prices are expensive, starting at ¥8,000. Listings magazines tell who is in town (► 92).

BLUE NOTE TOKYO

➕ E7 ✉ 5-13-3 Minami-Aoyama, Minato-ku
☎ 3407–5781
🚇 Omotesando

POP & ROCK CONCERTS

Local and visiting stars perform at the Tokyo Dome (► 84), and on summer evenings outdoors in Hibiya Park (► 42). Another indoor venue is:

NIPPON BUDOKAN HALL

The martial arts arena built for the 1964 Olympics.
➕ J4 ✉ 2-3 Kitanomaru Koen, Chiyoda-ku ☎ 3216–5100 🚇 Kudanshita

MOVIES

Most films come from Hollywood and are shown with the original soundtracks and Japanese subtitles. Smaller "boutique" cinemas screen later performances and provide an infinitely varied diet, including classics, reruns and European movies. Tickets are around ¥1,800. For a little more money you can reserve seats. Check the listings in the local English-language publications (► 92).

CENTRAL TICKET AGENCIES

For most theaters, concert halls and major sports arenas, you can reserve tickets up to the day before the performance at agencies such as:

Kyukyodo

➕ K7 ✉ 5-7-4 Ginza, Chuo-ku ☎ 3571–4429
🚇 Higashi-Ginza

Play Guide Honten

➕ K6 ✉ 2-6-4 Ginza, Chuo-ku ☎ 3561–8821 🚇 Ginza
On the day of the performance, telephone the venue and arrange to collect the tickets there; if you have a problem making yourself understood, ask someone at your hotel to make the call.

Entertainment Districts

MEETING POINT

Everyone in Tokyo knows the statue of Hachiko, an Akita dog who used to walk with his master, a university professor, to Shibuya Station each morning, and meet him off the train again in the evening. One day in 1925, the professor did not return: He had suddenly been taken ill and died. Hachiko waited for the last train and then sadly made his way home. For seven years, he came every evening to wait, until at last he too died. Touched by such loyalty, the people of Tokyo paid for the bronze statue outside the station.

"Like calls to like" is the Japanese equivalent of "birds of a feather," and it certainly applies to Tokyo's nightspots. The crowds go where the action is, so ever more places open up in these areas in order to tap the market.

AKASAKA

Two parallel streets, Hitotsugi-dori and Tamachi-dori, and the narrow alleyways between them are packed with bars, clubs and restaurants. It's respectable and rather expensive, although not quite in the Ginza league, and mostly frequented by company men on expense accounts and people staying at the area's big hotels.

GINZA

The prices in the clubs and top restaurants are legendary, and prohibitive for anyone not on an unlimited expense account. Others can enjoy the street scene, find a fast-food or budget restaurant and enjoy a drink in one of the afford-able bars or big beer halls.

IKEBUKURO

The streets around Ikebukuro Station, particularly the west side, have a vibrant night-life and are popular with shoppers at the weekend. The crowds here are more diverse than, say, Ginza, and it is a great district to come face-to-face with a cross-section of Toyoites. It is one of the most densely populated areas of the city.

ROPPONGI

This is a favorite with Tokyo's foreign contingent as well as more adventurous Japanese, partly because it's still awake at 4am, while elsewhere has quietened down by midnight. The Almond coffee house at the main street crossing near the subway station is a popular rendezvous and landmark. There's a huge choice of eating and drinking places nearby, but prices have risen in recent years to rival Akasaka levels. Drunks may be a problem in a few bars and discos.

SHIBUYA

Busy and cheerful, with a mainly young crowd, this popular stopping and entertainment district is not as expensive as Akasaka. There's a host of fast-food outlets and a wide choice of ethnic restaurants. Local groups play in the live music bars.

SHINJUKU

As the gateway to the city from the west, Shinjuku has always entertained travelers. The railroad gave it a boost, and Kabukicho northeast of the station is Japan's biggest red-light district. From respectable bars and fine restaurants, the nightlife runs the range, testing the limits of legality. Women in miniskirts hand out addresses and prices of massage parlors; hard-faced barkers urge passers-by to see strip shows and bottomless bars.

Other Ideas

A night out can be costly, unless you are being entertained by local business contacts, who will expect to pick up the tab (you can return the hospitality when they visit your home country). You are not likely to be invited to a Japanese home until you know someone very well; Anyway most people eat out more than they do at home.

LOCAL CHOICES

Robatayaki restaurants are cheerful, noisy places where varied foods are cooked on an open grill amid clouds of smoke. A *ryori-ya* or *shokudo* is a mixed-menu restaurant: plastic replicas in the window show the choices and prices. *Chuka ryori-ya* are basic Chinese restaurants, often visited by Japanese families for a cheap meal, serving such staples as fried rice and noodle dishes. *Ramen-ya* and *soba-ya* serve inexpensive bowls of noodles in a soup or with a topping. A *kissaten* is a coffee house serving light snacks and sweet pastries—the coffee may be expensive but you can sit as long as you like. For a moderately priced breakfast of toast, coffee, a boiled egg and small salad, ask for *moningu sabisu* ("morning service").

BARS

The variety is endless. Take a look inside and decide if the atmosphere appeals to you. If prices are not posted, ask for a list. Bottles of good French or Australian wine start from about ¥2,000. Beers run from ¥500 to ¥800 or more. The good, if rather bland, local whiskey costs much less than imported brands. Bars and clubs where local or western groups perform ("live houses") generally make an extra charge of ¥1,000–1,500. A *nomi-ya* is a small informal neighborhood bar, also known as *akachochin*, and indicated by the red lantern outside, which often sell snacks. *Karaoke* bars have spread round the world like wildfire but this is where the idea of amateur singing to a tape was born. Unless you want to fork out a large fee (¥5,000 an hour is typical), avoid bars where a hostess sits with you while you have an outrageously expensive drink (in less legitimate places other services could also be suggested).

DISCOS

Most are in Shibuya, Shinjuku and especially Roppongi, where the Square Building alone houses discos on most of its ten floors. It is impossible to predict from day to day which will be jumping and which empty or closed for good. Ask local contacts and check listings magazines (► 92). A cover charge about ¥4,500 includes a couple of drink tickets. The downside of the disco scene is the growth of aggressive behaviour, fueled by alcohol. When the atmosphere turns nasty, it is best to leave and find somewhere else.

BEER HALLS

These big, informal places, vaguely modeled on German *bierkeller,* are mostly run by the brewery companies. You sit at large or small tables, or bar counters, and order beers and plates of savory snacks— three or four add up to a meal. In addition, many department stores turn their roofs into beer gardens during the sultry summers. Top beer halls include:

Beer Station Sapporo
✚ E10 ✉ Yebisu Garden Place, 3 Ebisu, Shibuya-ku
Ⓔ Ebisu

Flamme d'Or Asahi
✚ Off map to northeast
✉ Asahi Brewery, 1 Azumabashi, Sumida-ku
Ⓔ Asakusa

Kirin City
✚ K6 ✉ Bunshodo Building 2F, 3-4-12 Ginza, Chuo-ku
Ⓔ Ginza

Sport & Sporting Venues

BIG STARS

For many years few foreigners undertook the rigorous training, let alone reached the senior ranks of *sumo*. The picture changed in the late 1980s when a Hawaiian known as Konishiki became a frequent winner. Then came an Irish-Polynesian, Akebono, who became the sole *yokozuna* (grand champion). The Japanese tolerated the invasion, while hoping for a home-grown hero, so there was relief at the promotion of Takanohana to *yokozuna* rank in 1994. Television has made *sumo* stars into national figures. More recently Mongolian sumo have reached the upper echelons of the sport. Most of the training stables are in Ryogoku, and some permit visitors to watch morning practice sessions between 5 and 10.30am. Get a Japanese speaker to make an appointment for you.
Azumazeki Stable
☎ 3624–0033
Kazugano Stable
☎ 3631–1871

SUMO

Literally "fat power," this form of wrestling was originally practiced at Shinto shrines and is surrounded by time-honored ceremony. After purification and other rituals, the two huge contenders collide, each intent on unbalancing the other and tipping him over or forcing him from the ring. *Basho* tournaments take place in January, May and September. Tickets for better seats are expensive, although they include a good box meal. Bouts are televised from 4 to 6pm each day of the tournament. The main Tokyo venue is:

KOKUGIKAN SUMO HALL
✚ N4 ✉ 1-3-28 Yokoami, Sumida-ku ☎ 3623–5111
🕐 10–6 (main bouts 3–6)
🚇 Ryogoku

BASEBALL

If there is a Japanese natural sport, this is it—top players and managers become media superstars. Tokyo has several teams in the two major leagues and one of them usually wins the Japan Series play-off. The season is from April to October, and the main venue is:

TOKYO DOME
This 55,000-seat stadium is where the baseball action is.
✚ J3 ✉ 1-3-61 Koraku, Bunkyo-ku ☎ 3811–2111
🚇 Suidobashi

GOLF

It seems as if half of Tokyo's businessmen claim to play and the game has a devoted following, but the it is expensive and the courses remote They console themselves at driving ranges, whose big net cages are a feature of the skyline.

TENNIS

Some big hotels have courts, even in Tokyo itself as do the Tokyo Bay resorts. Hibiya Park (► 42) in the city center has public courts. Tennis has popular local participation.

SWIMMING

The nearest reasonably clean beach is at Enoshima near Kamakura (► 20), which is crowded, especially at weekends, from June to the end of August, and deserted the rest of the year. Toshima-en amusement park (► 64) has several swimming pools; Yoyogi Park's sports center has a large one, but it's often in use for events.

PLACES TO JOG

Traffic pollution and sidewalk congestion make the streets a less than enjoyable place to jog, but there's a park within easy reach of most hotels. Best of all is the Imperial Palace East Garden (► 38). Shinjuku has its "Central Park" (► 30). Many big hotels provide jogging maps.

Bath Houses

The earth's crust seems especially thin in Japan. The unstable ground threatens disaster in the form of earthquakes and *tsunami* and creates countless hot springs. Tokyo is no exception. Coffee-colored, mineral-rich water from beneath the city is piped to dozens of *onsen* (hot spring-fed baths); other public baths are called *sento*. They traditionally served as community centers where local people gathered to relax, and in older parts of the city they still do. These days, the sexes are generally segregated: Only in some open-air rural spas is there mixed bathing. Three traditional *onsen* in Tokyo are:

ASAKUSA KANNON ONSEN

A large and very hot bath esteemed for its curative properties.

➕ N2 ✉ 2-7-26 Asakusa 2, Taito-ku ☎ 3844–4141
🕐 Daily 6.30am–6.30pm
Ⓜ Asakusa

AZABU JUBAN ONSEN

A cosy *onsen*, in an unlikely location, the third floor of a modern building.

➕ G8 ✉ 1-5-22 Azabu Juban, Minato-ku ☎ 3404–2610
🕐 Wed–Mon 11–9
Ⓜ Roppongi

SUEHIRO BUSINESS HOTEL

Very hot natural spring bath with sauna and steam room.

➕ Off map to west
✉ 8-1-5 Nishikamata, Ota-ku
☎ 3734–6561 🕐 Daily
6am–9pm, 1–midnight
Ⓜ Kamata

ORDER OF THE BATH

• On entering, take off all your clothes in the changing room.
• Take only your towel, soap and shampoo into the bath room.
• Sit on one of the stools away from the bath.
• Douse yourself with water using a scoop, bucket or shower, set in the wall at knee height, whatever is provided.
• Wash thoroughly all over and meticulously rinse off all the soap. *No trace of soap must get into the bath itself.*
• Immerse yourself gradually in the bath (*ofuro*). If there's a choice, try the less hot bath first. Temperatures typically range from 108°F (42°C) up to about 118°F (48°C).
• Don't put your head underwater.
• If you feel dizzy get out.
• Some users recommend getting in and out several times.
• Don't drink alcohol before the bath.

If you're staying in a private house, much the same rules apply. Replace the cover on the bath to keep the water hot for other users. In a *ryokan* (► 88), which may have a bath for couples or families as well as the men's and women's, the maid will usually ask you when you would like to take your bath, and come to let you know when it is ready. The accepted bath time in a *ryokan* or private home is before the evening meal.

RITUAL

The Shinto code emphasizes purity and cleanliness, not only of the mind but of the body. Faith and medical research agree that a hot, deep bath is beneficial to health, reducing stress and tension and relieving aches and pains.

"Soaplando" massage parlors are less concerned with the spiritual element—the masseuses coat their own bodies and the client's with lather before getting to work. Confirm prices and exact services offered before you go too far in one of these establishments.

Luxury Hotels

WHAT YOU PAY FOR

The cost of a double room per night, with private bath (except for *ryokan* and hostels), excluding breakfast:

Luxury: over ¥30,000
Mid-range: ¥18,000–¥30,000
Budget: up to ¥18,000

Tokyo deserves its reputation for high prices, but the top hotels are no more expensive than the equivalent in New York, London or Frankfurt. Take into account the standard of service, facilities and impeccable cleanliness, and they might be considered good value. Almost all Japanese hotels provide toothbrushes, toothpaste, a razor and shaving cream and a cotton *yukata* (robe).

LOST IN TOKYO

Fan s of *Lost in Translation* could check out the Park Hyatt Tokyo, where much of the film's story took place. A visit to the New York Bar for a night-time drink is like stepping onto the movie set.

ANA HOTEL TOKYO

A 37-story, 903-room block with a sober exterior and lots of marble in the Ark Hills area, between Roppongi and Akasaka. Health club, pool, executive floor and restaurants.
✚ H7 ✉ 1-12-33 Akasaka, Minato-ku ☎ 3505–1111, fax 3505–1155; www.anahotels.com /tokyo/e 🚇 Tameike-sanno

HOTEL NIKKO TOKYO

This waterfront urban resort, part of the Tokyo Bay area redevelopment (► 49), has 453 harbour-view rooms, eight restaurants, two bars and a pool.
✚ Off map to south ✉ 1-9-1 Daiba, Minato-ku ☎ 5500–5500, fax 5500–2525; www.hnt.jp/english 🚇 Daiba (Yurikamome line)

HOTEL OKURA TOKYO

Stately and formal, this is one of the first of the postwar grand hotels, with 858 rooms, restaurants, an art gallery and indoor and outdoor pools.
✚ H7 ✉ 2-10-4 Toranomon, Minato-ku ☎ 3582–0111, fax 3582–3707; www. hotelokura.co.jp 🚇 Toranomon

IMPERIAL

A city-within-a-city, in the heart of Ginza and facing Hibiya Park. The 1,059 rooms are beautifully appointed, with superb views from upper floors. Over 20 restaurants, dozens of stores, a health club and pool.
✚ J6 ✉ 1-1-1 Uchisaiwaicho, Chiyoda-ku ☎ 3504–1111, fax 3581–9146; www.imperialhotel.co.jp 🚇 Hibiya

NEW OTANI

One of Tokyo's very best—the surrounding Japanese garden is worth a visit. Super luxury. There are many stores and over 30 restaurants. 1,600 rooms.
✚ G5 ✉ 4-1 Kioi-cho, Chiyoda-ku ☎ 3265–1111, fax 3221–2619; www.newotani.co.jp 🚇 Akasaka-mitsuke

PARK HYATT TOKYO

On the 39th to 52nd floors of a pyramid-topped glass tower at the western edge of Shinjuku. An elegant and spacious hotel with 178 rooms, 3 restaurants and a rooftop swimming pool.
✚ C5 ✉ 3-7-1-2 Nishi-Shinjuku, Shinjuku-ku ☎ 5322–1234, fax 5322–1288; www.parkhyatttokyo.com 🚇 Shinjuku

TOKYO PRINCE HOTEL

Large rooms, a splendid location, top facilities and attentive service are probably the main reasons for choosing this 484-room luxury hotel.
✚ J8 ✉ 3-3-1 Shibakoen, Minato-ku ☎ 3432–1111, fax 3434–5551; www.princehotelsjapan.com 🚇 Onarimon

WESTIN TOKYO

A stylish hotel with richly decorated public areas and 445 guest rooms, part of an entertainment and shopping complex on the former Sapporo Brewery site.
✚ E10 ✉ Yebisu Garden Place, 1-4-1 Mita, Meguro-ku ☎ 5423–7000, fax 5423–7600; www.westin.co.jp 🚇 Ebisu

Mid-Range Hotels

CROWNE PLAZA METROPOLITAN

Three minutes' walk from Ikebukuro station, this 815-room well-appointed hotel has a gym and pool.

✚ Off map to northwest ✉ 1-6-1 Nishi-Ikebukuro, Toshima-ku ☎ 3980–1111, fax 3980–8505; www.itbc.co.jp/hotel 🚇 Ikebukuro

GINZA CAPITAL HOTEL

A basic business hotel with 574 compact rooms, close to Tsukiji subway station, reasonably convenient to Ginza.

✚ L7 ✉ 3-1-9 Tsukiji, Chuo-ku ☎ 3543–8211, fax 3543–7839; www.ginza-capital.co.jp/en 🚇 Tsukiji

GINZA NIKKO

While the 112 rooms may be small, the location, not far from central Ginza, makes this the shopper's choice of accommodations.

✚ J7 ✉ 8-4-21 Ginza, Chuo-ku ☎ 3571–4911, fax 3571–8379; www.nikkohotels.com 🚇 Shimbashi

HOTEL IBIS

A business hotel with 182 rooms and above average style close to Roppongi. Busy at weekends.

✚ G7 ✉ 7-14-4 Roppongi, Minato-ku ☎ 3403–4411, fax 3479–0609;www.ibis-hotel.com/index-e.htm 🚇 Roppongi

RIHGA ROYAL HOTEL KYOTO

Just 7 minutes' walk from Kyoto station, this 598-room quality hotel includes a roof-top French restaurant.

✚ Kyoto ✉ Horikawa-Shiokoji, Kyoto ☎ 075–341–1121, fax 075–341–3073; www.rihga-kyoto.co.jp 🚇 Kyoto

ROPPONGI PRINCE

Compact 216-room hotel close to Roppongi. Courtyard with a café and swimming pool.

✚ H7 ✉ 3-2-7 Roppongi, Minato-ku ☎ 3587–1111, fax 3587–0770; www.princehotels japan.com 🚇 Roppongi

SHINJUKU NEW CITY

Your average mid-range hotel with 400 good size rooms. Just to the west of Shinjuku station.

✚ D4 ✉ 4-31-1 Nishi-Shinjuku, Shinjuku-ku ☎ 3375–6511, fax 3375–6535; www.newcityhotel.co.jp 🚇 Tochomae

STAR HOTEL TOKYO

A small, functional but friendly hotel with 80 rooms, only two-minute walk from Shinjuku Station and the entertainment district.

✚ D4 ✉ 7-10-5 Nishi-Shinjuku, Shinjuku-ku ☎ 3361–1111, fax 3369–4216; www.starhotel.co.jp 🚇 Shinjuku

SUN HOTEL SHINBASHI

A central-area business hotel, 3 minutes' walk from Shinbashi JR or subway stations, one stop away from central Ginza. 233 rooms.

✚ J7 ✉ 3-5-2 Shinbashi, Minato-ku ☎ 3591–3351, fax 3592–1977; www.sun-hotel.co.jp 🚇 Shinbashi

TOKYO STATION

An old-fashioned hotel in part of the historic station building, completed in 1914. Of the 170 rooms, 56 have a bath.

✚ K5 ✉ 1-9-1 Marunouchi, Chiyoda-ku ☎ 3231–2511, fax 3231–3513; www.tshl.co.jp 🚇 Tokyo

THE BARE ESSENTIALS

Many places in the mid-range category are "business hotels," providing a small room and tiny bathroom, telephone, TV and perhaps an in-house restaurant. The main difference between these and other hotels is their good location. Facilities vary, but most offer internet access and room service.

Budget Accommodations

OTHER OPTIONS

Capsule hotels accommodate you in stacked boxes, often likened to coffins. At about 3ft x 3ft x 6ft (1m x 1m x 2m), they are not for sufferers of claustrophobia. The majority are strictly for men only, mainly those who have partied too long and missed the last train home.

"Love hotels" give couples a chance to be alone together—their success is a direct result of a lack of living space for Tokyoites who often share space with extended families. Rooms are usually rented by the hour, or two; after 10pm an economy all-night rate applies. Love hotels tend to be concentrated in the entertainment districts such as Shibuya, Ikebukuro, East Shinjuku or Roppongi. Rooms can be elaborately decorated; photos of them are proudly displayed at the entrance.

ASIA CENTER OF JAPAN

A rare budget hotel, with 172 plain, Western-style rooms, some with a private bath. Cafeteria. Reserve well in advance.

⊕ H7 ✉ 8-10-32 Akasaka, Minato-ku ☎ 3402–6111, fax 3402–0738 🚇 Aoyama-itchome

HOTEL ALCYONE

A Stellar near-Ginza location makes up for the tiny rooms of this 74-room Western-style business hotel.

⊕ L7 ✉ 4-14-3 Ginza, Chuo-ku ☎ 3541–3621, fax 3541–3262; email hotelalcyone@msn.com 🚇 Higashi-Ginza

YMCA ASIA YOUTH CENTER

Both sexes are welcome. 55 rooms, some with private bath. Seven or eight minutes on foot from Suidobashi or Jinbocho.

⊕ J3 ✉ 2-5-5 Saragakucho, Chiyoda-ku ☎ 3233–0611, fax 3233–0633 🚇 Suidobashi 🚇 Jinbocho

RYOKAN

The traditional Japanese lodging, *ryokan*, can be expensive and are often reluctant to take foreigners. Rooms normally have *tatami* (mats) and *futon* bedding (a thin mattress and quilt), which is rolled up until evening. A few have Western-style rooms too.

KIMI RYOKAN

This friendly little place with 35 Japanese-style rooms is popular with Westerners and often full. Seven minutes' walk north-west of Ikebukuro Station.

⊕ Off map ✉ 2-36-8 Ikebukuro, Toshima-ku ☎ 3971–3766, fax 3987–1326; www.kimi-ryokan.jp 🚇 Ikebukuro

SAKURA RYOKAN

Close to Ueno and Asakusa, with 12 Japanese-style and 8 Western-style rooms.

⊕ M1 ✉ 2-6-2 Iriya, Taito-ku ☎ 3876–8118, fax 3873–9456; www.sakura-ryokan.com/index-en.htm 🚇 Iriya

SAWANOYA RYOKAN

A modern inn with 12 Japanese-style rooms, close to Ueno Park in the old Yanaka neighborhood. Free internet.

⊕ K1 ✉ 2-3-11 Yanaka, Taito-ku ☎ 3822–2251, fax 3822–2252; www.sawanoya.com 🚇 Nezu

HOSTELS

Expensive by international standards, hostels are often full. Try to reserve well in advance. There's no age restriction, but if you don't belong to any Youth Hostel Association you may be charged extra.

TOKYO INTERNATIONAL YOUTH HOSTEL

Simple dormitory-style accommodations in a modern tower-block. Advance reservations required. 33 rooms.

⊕ H3 ✉ Central Plaza 18F, 1-1 Kaguragashi, Shinjuku-ku ☎ 3235–1107, fax 3267–4000 🚇 Iidabashi

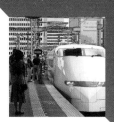

TOKYO
travel facts

ESSENTIAL FACTS

Customs regulations
- Duty-free allowances are 200 cigarettes or 50 cigars, 3 x 750ml bottles of liquor, 57g perfume, ¥200,000 worth of gifts.

Electricity
- 100V AC, 50Hz. US 110V equipment will operate. Plugs have two flat, parallel pins.

Etiquette
- Japanese custom is to bow when meeting someone. A handshake will be accepted, but an attempt to follow custom and give a bow will be appreciated.
- When visiting a Japanese home, bring a present, ideally something unusual from your own country.
- Shoes must be removed before entering a home, a *ryokan*, many shrine halls and some restaurants. Slippers are usually provided, but it will save embarrassment if your socks are free from holes.
- Visiting cards are exchanged at every opportunity. If you are on business, take a large supply. They should state your position in your organization. If possible, have a translation in Japanese characters printed on the reverse. Hotels can arrange this quickly. When given a card, study it with interest; do not put it away unread.
- For table etiquette (➤ 67, panel).
- It is not usual to tip in Japan, except for special extra services. A 10–15 percent service charge is added to hotel and some restaurant bills. Porters charge a set fee.

Finding an address
- Few streets have names, and even these are rarely used in addresses. Even taxi drivers have trouble.

- Building numbers generally relate to the order of construction, not to position.
- In a Tokyo address such as 3-10-2 Akasaka (the district), Minato-ku (city ward), 3 is the subdivision or *chome* and 10-2 the building. 'F' means floor; ground level is 1F. A map pinpointing the place and related landmarks is essential.

Lavatories
- Hotels have the western type; some even an optional "paperless" mode with warm water jets and hot air to clean your underside.
- The Japanese version, in most public lavatories, is at ground level with no seat. You squat over it, facing the flushing handle. Carry your own paper.
- Department stores usually have both versions. Not all public lavatories are segregated.

Money matters
- Travelers' checks in yen may be used instead of cash. Those in other currencies can be changed at banks or at hotels, where the exchange rate may not be quite as good. A passport is needed.
- Major credit cards are accepted by most hotels, big stores and many restaurants, but rarely by smaller ones or fast-food outlets. It is still essential, and safe, to carry cash. Telephones and ticket-vending machines take 10, 50 and 100 yen coins.
- ATMs outside banks will take some cards. Check with card issuers to see which are accepted.

National holidays
- If a national holiday falls on a Sunday, the Monday following is a holiday.
- January 1: New Year's Day;

Second Monday in January:
Coming of Age Day for 20-year-olds.
- February 11: Foundation Day.
- March 20 or 21: Vernal Equinox Day.
- April 29: Greenery Day.
- May 3: Constitution Day;
4: National Holiday;
5: Children's Day.
- September 15: Respect for the Aged Day;
23 or 24: Autumn Equinox Day.
- October 10: Health in Sports Day.
- November 3: Culture Day;
23: Labour Day.
- 23 December: Emperor's Birthday.

Opening hours
- Shops: Mon–Sat 10–6, 7 or 8.
- Banks: Mon–Fri 9–3.
- Offices: Mon–Fri 9–5 (businesses work half day on Sat).
- Museums: Tue–Sun 10, 10.30 or 11–4 or 5. (Closed Tue if Mon a national holiday.)

Places of worship
The following have services in English, call for details:
- Roman Catholic: Franciscan Chapel Center ✉ 4-2-37 Roppongi, Minato-ku ☎ 3401-2141
- Protestant: Tokyo Bapist ✉ 9-2 Hachiyama-cho, Shibuya-ku ☎ 3461-8425
- Jewish: Jewish Community Centre ✉ 3-8-8 Hiroo, Shibuya-ku ☎ 3400-2559
- Islamic: Tokyo Mosque ✉ 1-16 Oyama-cho, Shibuya-ku ☎ 5790-0760
- Interdenominational: Tokyo Union Church ✉ 5-7-7 Jingu-mae, Shibuya-ku ☎ 3400-0047

GETTING AROUND

Buses
- Make sure you know the route number, and it is best to have your destination written down in Japanese to show people when asking for help.
- On boarding, passengers take a numbered ticket. The fare is shown on an electronic display and paid on leaving the bus.

The Metro
- At the station, find the row of ticket machines for that line. Price lists are displayed nearby. If you cannot find one, buy the lowest price ticket and pay any extra at your destination at "Fare Adjustment" machines.
- Machines give change.
- Feed the ticket face up into the entry gate and collect it when the machine expels it. It is essential that you keep it until the ride is over.
- Follow signs to the line and platform (track) you need, some-times identified by the final station on the line. Stand at the yellow markers, if there are any passengers on the train, wait to one side before boarding.
- At each stop, signs give the sta-tion's name and that of the next in Japanese and Roman script.
- At your destination, find an exit directory (a yellow board); note the number of the exit you want before going through the ticket gate. Otherwise you'll walk vast distances and probably get lost.
- Travel light at rush hour. There are many stairs, and long walks to exits or when you are transferring between lines.

Taxis
- It is best to show an area map with your destination marked.
- Pay only the fare on the meter. Tipping is not expected.

Trains

- The JR has an English-language telephone service ☎ 3423–0111

Where to get maps

- Larger hotels give out excellent city and subway maps; large stations supply subway maps.
- For both leaflets and maps, visit the Tourist Information Centers (TICs) run by JNTO at ✉ Narita Airport Terminal 2, and in the city center at ➕ K6 ✉ 10F Tokyo Kotosukaikan Building, 2-10-1 Yurakucho, Chiyoda-ku ☎ 3201–3331 ◷ Mon–Fri 9–5, Sat 9–noon; closed Dec 29–Jan 1 Ⓔ Yurakucho
- TTIC ➕ C4 ✉ 1F Tokyo Metropolitan Government Building, No 1 Shinjuku ☎ 5321–3077 ◷ Daily 9.30–6.30 Ⓔ Tochomae

MEDIA & COMMUNICATIONS

International newsdealers

- A full range of foreign magazines is stocked at news-stands in big hotels and major train stations, and in large bookstores (▶ 78).

Listings magazines

- The quarterly *Tokyo Journal* has full listings of exhibitions, markets, services and entertainment. Restaurant, club and bar reviews may be biased to advertisers.

Newspapers

- There are four English-language translations of the main Japanese dailies: the *Japan Times*, *Daily Yomiuri*, *Mainichi Daily News* and *Asahi Evening News*.

Post offices

- Hotel desks are the most convenient place to post letters and cards. They have stamps and are familiar with postal rates.
- Go to post offices only to send heavy packages or registered mail. Staff can read Roman script.
- Post offices open Mon–Fri 9–5.
- 24-hour post office: Tokyo International Post Office ✉ 2-3-3 Otemachi, Chiyoda-ku

Telephones

- Coin- and card-operated phones are prevalent. Local calls cost ¥10 per minute. ¥500 or ¥1,000 cards are sold at hotels, airports, station kiosks and machines near phones.
- Make international direct-dial calls from gray and green phones with a gold front panel, card phones, or phones marked "international". Use only ¥100 coins, or cards. Several companies compete, each having its own international access code. Dial 0057 (for KDDI), 0088–41 (ITJ) or 0061 (IDC), followed by the country code, area code (omit any initial 0), and number. The calling card codes of other international companies can also be used. MCI ☎ 0039–121 or 0066–55–121; AT&T ☎ 0039–111 or 0066–55–111
- Direct dialling from hotel rooms is expensive.
- Dial 0051 for person-to-person and collect (reverse charge) calls, and 0057 (toll-free) for information.
- Mobile phones from other countries are not compatible with Japanese networks.

EMERGENCIES

Emergency phone numbers

- Police ☎ 110
- Fire and Ambulance ☎ 119
- Emergency numbers are toll-free. On pay phones push the red button first.
- There are police boxes (*koban*) on

many street corners and resident police in every little district. They usually speak only Japanese.

Embassies

- Australia ✉ 2-1-14 Mita, Minato-ku, Tokyo 108 ☎ 5232–4111
- Canada ✉ 7-3-38 Akasaka, Minato-ku, Tokyo 107 ☎ 5412–6200
- Germany ✉ 4-5-10 Minami-azabu, Minato-ku, 106 ☎ 3473–0151
- Netherlands ✉ 3-6-3 Shiba-koen, Minato-ku, 10 ☎ 5401–0411
- New Zealand ✉ 20-40 Kamiyama-cho, Shibuya-ku, Tokyo 150 ☎ 3467–2271
- UK ✉ 1 Ichiban-cho, Chiyoda-ku, Tokyo 102 ☎ 5211–1100
- USA ✉ 1-10-5 Akasaka, Minato-ku, Tokyo 107 ☎ 3224–5000

Lost property

- Tokyo Metro ☎ 3834–5577; TOEI lines: ☎ 3812–2011; JR trains ☎ 3231–1880 (Tokyo Station) ☎ 3841–8069 (Ueno Station)
- Taxis: ☎ 3648–0300
- Buses: ☎ 3818–5760

Medical treatment

- Standards—and costs—are high.
- Your embassy can recommend hospitals with some doctors who speak English.
- International Medical Information Center Toyko ☎ 5285–8088

Medication

- For prescription and non-prescription medication, when you need an English speaker: American Pharmacy ✚ K6 ✉ Hibiya Park Building 1-8-1 Yurakucho, Chiyodu-ku ☎ 3271–4034 🕒 Mon–Sat 9–8, Sun 10–6.30 Ⓢ Ginza

Sensible precautions

- Tokyo is the safest of the world's big cities to walk around. Even in the raunchier areas, such as

Kabukicho, you need not be too apprehensive.
- Use hotel safes for storing large sums of money.
- Streets and subways are safe but always exercise caution when walking at night.

LANGUAGE

- Romanized versions of Japanese words are more or less phonetic, so say the words as written.
- Give all syllables equal weight, except: 'u' at the end of a word, which is hardly sounded at all; 'i' in the middle of a word, which is skipped over, as in mash'te for mashite.
- E sounds like 'eh' in ten; g is generally hard, as in go.
- Two adjoining consonants are sounded separately.
- A dash over a vowel lengthens the vowel sound.
- Family names are now usually written second.

Useful words & phrases

How do you do? Hajime-mashite?
Good morning Ohayo gozai-masu
Good afternoon Kon-nichi-wa
Good evening Konban-wa
Good night Oyasumi-nasai
Goodbye Sayo-nara
Mr, Mrs, Miss, Ms -san (suffix to family name, or given name of friends)
Thank you Domo/arigato
Excuse me, sorry Sumi-masen
Please (when offering) Dozo
Please (when asking) Kudasai
Hello (telepone) Moshi-moshi
Yes Hai
Do you understand? Wakari-masu-ka?
Do you speak English? Eigo o hanashi-masu-ka?
Where is …? … wa doko desu-ka?

93

Index

Fodor's
tokyo's 25 best

AUTHOR *Martin Gostelow*
EDITION REVISER AND CONTRIBUTIONS TO 'LIVING TOKYO' *Rod Ritchie*
MANAGING EDITORS *Apostrophe S Limited*
COVER DESIGN *Tigist Getachew, Fabrizio La Rocca*

ISBN 14000-1636-3

FIFTH EDITION

ACKNOWLEDGMENTS
The Automobile Association would like to thank the following photographers, libraries and agencies for their assistance in the preparation of this title.
Alamy 31b; Martin Gostelow 37, 62; Japanese National Tourist Organisation 64; Courtesy of Mori Art Museum 33t, 33b (photo by Koiku Keizo); National Museum of Modern Art 39b; Ota Memorial Museum of Art 54; Spectrum Colour Library 28, 30t, 38, 40t, 41, 42b, 43, 51b, 57; Stockbyte 5; Suntory Museum 55; Tokyo Convention and Visitors Bureau 34t, 36b, 49, 50t, 50b, 56; World Pictures 31t
The remaining photographs are held in the Association's own library (AA WORLD TRAVEL LIBRARY) and were take by Jim Holmes with the exception of 39t, 44b which were taken by R T Alford; cover: Stark Building, 8/9, 9c, 10b, 18/19, 19cr, 20tr, 20c, 21, 24b, 25c, 26cr, 29t, 32, 47, 48, 51t, 61 which were taken by Douglas Corrance; and 17t which was taken by Phil Wood.

IMPORTANT TIP
Time inevitably brings changes, so always confirm prices, travel facts, and other perishable information when it matters. Although Fodor's cannot accept responsibility for errors, you can use this guide in the confidence that we have taken every care to ensure its accuracy.

SPECIAL SALES
This book is available for special discounts for bulk purchases for sales promotions or premiums. Special editions, including personalized covers, excerpts of existing books, and corporate imprints, can be created in large quantities for special needs. For more information, write to Special Markets/Premium Sales, 1745 Broadway, MD 6–2, New York, NY 10019 or email specialmarkets@randomhouse.com.

Colour separation by Keenes, Andover
Printed and bound in Hong Kong by Hang Tai D&P Limited
10 9 8 7 6 5 4 3 2 1

AO2353
Maps © Automobile Association Developments Limited 1996, 1999, 2001, 2002, 2006
Fold out map © MAIRDUMONT /Falk Verlag 2005
Transport map © Communicarta Ltd, UK

DESTINATIONS COVERED IN THIS SERIES
• Amsterdam • Bangkok • Barcelona • Beijing • Berlin • Boston • Brussels & Bruges •
• Chicago • Dublin • Florence • Hong Kong • Istanbul • Las Vegas • Lisbon • Ljubljana •
• London • Los Angeles • Madrid • Melbourne • Miami • Montréal • Munich • New York •
• Orlando • Paris • Prague • Rome • San Francisco • Seattle • Shanghai • Singapore •
• Sydney • Tokyo • Toronto • Venice • Vienna • Washington DC •